Riding
"The Midnight Hour"

Drama, excitement and fun
on the footplate
1914-54

When we rode the blackest night
Dark eyed and crying out for sleep
We thought of you who slept the night away

Oh how we envied you.

But when, on scented breeze, we rode the moonlight hour
Watched, bright eyed, the willow grove
Mood shadow on the reedy stream and magic all around

Oh how we pitied you.

Geoff Brown

CONTENTS

PREFACE

I worked on the railway from 1941 to 1954. I began as an engine cleaner come general labourer at Oxley, and had reached the stage of Top Spare Link fireman, at Stafford Rd when I left. This Link covered the crews of the top express trains when the fireman was sick, on holidays, or off for any reason. In addition, we had several express jobs in our own right.

In the course of moving from cleaner to senior fireman I had been assistant to the brick archer for at least a year. After that, as we became firemen, we all worked at Oxley or Stafford rd sheds, filling any space that became vacant as we moved up through the links.

The job of fireman was a good one. If you could get on with your mate, the driver, and I usually could, it was a splendid job.

Every day brought a different task, until you had worked every job in the link. The link was a group of jobs of similar importance right around the clock. You soon got to know the guards, the shunters, the other loco men who you would work with or relieve, or would relieve you. They came from Crewe, Chester, Shrewsbury, Banbury, Tyseley and so on. It was a job full of fun, with rich characters whose, sometimes strange, ways made them the subject of endless small adventures. Long before you could get bored with the jobs in one link, there would be another link and another mate with more important jobs and yet more rich characters to spice the days and nights.

In the course of the daily and weekly tour of the Link we learned practically everything about each other. In fact it was almost impossible not to, if your own mate didn't tell you, someone else would. We found ourselves with no other company on countless occasions. Sometimes sitting on the opposite sides of the footplate, occupying a non corridor compartment, or some lonely cabin. It could be day or night, summer or winter, a glorious spring day or a biting wicked winters night. It mattered not, we were bound to talk, and in talking to learn more and more about each others lives.

Some men were open and talkative, while others spoke rarely, but either way, over weeks and months you were bound to learn a great deal about each other. Oh how I wish I had written down the countless stories, made note of the strange sayings which laced the conversation of many men. How I have regretted not refreshing my memory and recording the details of the many rich characters who abounded among the footplate men all over the Great Western.

Twelve long years passed, and I was too busy enjoying it all to think of recording them. The memories have faded and the details grown shadowy over these past 40 years. Some of the names of men who I knew so well have gone completely, and so, in many cases have the details of their lives and the yarns they told.

Even so, since deciding to record what I can of those days I have met with and talked with some of those men and made many recordings in an effort to stake down some of those fleeting memories that will soon be gone for ever, because the youngest of us who can recall those times are retired by now. Luckily, the human mind does not lose it's memories as finally and completely as I had imagined and once I started talking again to the men I once knew, and staring again at pictures of engines, places and sometimes men, who I had known long ago, the memories began creeping back. Of course there is much that has gone for ever, but there are men and stories that I could never forget. The men I mated for months, the things which happened to us, the the most memorable yarns they told, or the yarns that were told to us, these will be there as long as I live.

For a long time I hesitated to take up the pen at all. I was afraid of getting the facts wrong after all this time. Afraid that my youthful memories might exaggerate or distort the facts. After all, any story that I can recall can almost certainly be recalled (often better) by someone else.

Eventually though, I realised that if I didn't record some of it, then maybe no one would, and that would be a great pity.

In the following pages, I have tried to show a little of the humour, the drama and sometimes the sheer stupidity that existed. I have also tried to cover the identities of those whose stories may embarrass them or their relatives by useing only nick-names or Christian names. The stories are not in chronological order, or any order really, they are just a few of the countless stories which could be told out of the experiences of myself and others.

My only purpose has been to record some of the events in the day to day activities of a unique and fascinating bunch of men.

I have tried to show just a little of the good and the bad, the drunkards and the gentlemen. All men who had been moulded by their tough upbringing and shaped by the unique job which occupied their lives.

They, and the powerful machines which they gave their lives to, changed Britain and it's people for ever, and now the massive organisation which they once served has gone, and nothing quite like it can ever come again.

THE JOB

We knew security. Every day, we were needed. There was a feeling of permanence, a feeling that we were part of an organisation which had an ever present and vital role in the life of the nation. The service provided, not only the essential requirements of life, food, fuel, the products and raw materials of industry, but also that exciting spice of life, passenger transport. In the days before the motor car became common place, a modest sum of money, well within the reach of most folk, would make it possible to board a train in Wolverhampton and alight with the sounds and the sights of the sea flooding our senses.

Moments after leaving Low Level you could be sliding swiftly past a panorama of hills and valleys, rivers and streams, the like of which were rarely seen by town dwellers before the railways came. A ticket, bought weeks or months in advance, provided endless hours of excited anticipation.

We, felt ourselves to be part of, and essential to, all that was best about the society in which we lived. We didn't go around thinking such thoughts, in fact some of us may never have thought such thoughts, but we felt them, the feelings came to work with us every day. They accompanied us, not only on good days but amongst the struggle and discomforts which were a part of our daily life. It was a feeling of total participation in something which was essentially good, manly, and totally worthwhile.

Where can a modern youth find such satisfaction today. This feeling permeated the structure of many of the larger essential industries in the second quarter of this century. We needed no television to entertain us. The conversation and antics of the odder members of our profession were entertainment enough. There was a certain degree of drama and danger which dogged our days but most of all there was humour. I find it impossible to write or even think of those days without instantly recalling the comics and the hilarious situations they created in an industry with more than it's fair share of eccentricity and often hypocrisy.

Through it all though, ran the dedication and skill which underlined a silent but sacred commitment to providing a safe and sure service and to be a 'Good Railwaymen'. All this began to slip away in the fifties with rationalization, reorganisation and the need for rapid turn over, and so on.

Now, there seems to be little or no sign of such feelings anywhere. Present day life may yield more consumer goods for some, but the taste and flavour of life has been diluted until they are hardly detectable

The real vital sense and flavour of those times exist only in our memories and we are lucky and privileged to have them.

SHOCK!

I suppose I'd been left the railway over twenty years when Charlie asked me to call at the sheds for him. In that twenty odd years I had seen very little of Stafford Road or Oxley Loco sheds. In fact, apart from a brief glimpse of Low Level Station on occasional day outings, I had not seen or thought much, at all, of the way of life which was once my daily preoccupation. For twenty years my thoughts and actions had been entirely concerned with the building trade. I had found this new world of drawings and pricing, of bricklaying, plastering, carpentry and so on; so completely absorbing that most of my previous life was submerged in a welter of new ideas and new ways.

Occasionally I would hear tit-bits of information about men that I knew and their doings. The press often reported changes that were taking place but to be honest, my new occupation was taking about twelve hours out of most days and with something new arising with every passing hour, I suppose it all went over my head.

Anyhow, Charlie had asked me to call at Stafford Rd to collect a steel drum which he had acquired to use as a water butt. He said it was just inside the little shed, so on my way back from town I stopped the van outside the small wooden doors which for years had been an important part of my life. I certainly knew that there had been some changes, but what changes! Through the doors, the familiar offices were empty; not just of people, empty of everything. On the wall on my right were the notice cases which used to be the focus of all our attentions. Gone were the names of those men we once knew, gone were the names of the engines we loved and hated and the lists of jobs which stretched around the clock and back again. Just the cases covered in dust, devoid of life; it was all a bit eerie.

I walked quickly across to the shed doors, anxious to have a last look. Then came the shock! The scene that was revealed was not one of change or even partial demolition, it was one of complete emptiness. My eyes met a great flat, open area that might have been a huge carpark or a levelled bomb site. Not one brick stood to show where Stafford Rd shed had been.

It was as if the entire shed and all it held had been wiped clean away before my very eyes. Gone was the turn-table with its' radiating roads that housed pannier tankys and side tankys galore. Gone the fitters cabin, the Forge, the Tool House, the Stores, the Boiler House.
The lower yard beyond was no more, no 'Castles' or 'Kings' stood over the firepits; no anything, just a derelict wasteland. No amount of staring in open-mouthed indignation would bring back one brick. I know it was stupid, I should have known. I should have expected it, but I didn't and it took me by surprise. As I staggered out with Charlie's oil drum I was absolutely stunned. After I'd stowed the drum away I went back for another look but it was a waste of time there was nothing to see.

As I started down Stafford Rd in the old van, I realised that it was not just my mind which had sustained a shock. Incredible though it seemed I knew that something deeper had been shaken. It seemed as if an old friend had died and been buried while I'd been too busy to notice. It was a bit annoying to be so affected by the removal of an old building. Of course, it wasn't the removal of an old building that had affected me so, it was all those men I'd known and the thriving, bustling organisation that had gone with them. An important slice of my past life had gone forever. Before I'd reached Charlie's place my mind had seen Stafford Rd shed in all its' glory. Suddenly it was all so vivid, I pictured it again as I always would at its most exciting time, the early hours of the morning.

Outside were the silent streets, the echoing pavements, the drawn curtains hiding the countless prostrate humans; people sleeping, uncaring while the world rolled on. But once through those dirty faceless shed doors the world was awake and active, a little subdued by the night maybe, but only a little. Just a pause, a catch of breath. Before the build up began. One engine after another would ring to the sound of studded boots on metal steps, the lids of metal tool boxes were being unlocked and everywhere was the rattle of fire irons as their masters for the day began to work.

Flare lamps came alight casting their flickering light into the dark corners of the foot plate. Drivers appeared at the store window wiping the oily muck from the oil bottles as they waited for their ration of oil and cotton waste. The blowers were on, the light from the fireholes became brighter by the minute. On the footplates the firemen worked in the blinding light and heat of the fire, drops of sweat turned to rivers as they struggled to break up two hundredweight lumps of Welsh steam coal jammed behind the steel tender doors. Broken into useable lumps, they hurled them into the roaring furnace, shielding their eyes from the blinding light by turning the shovel first one way then another to see that every part of the 4 foot by 12 foot 6 inch firebox was evenly covered until about 18 inches of coal was being eaten into by the raging flames.

This would slowly build to the inferno needed to sustain steam while the engine blasted 14 eight-wheelers from a stand to high speed in less than a minute. As they worked, the safety valves lifted. An ominous hiss grew into an indescribably deafening roar; men passed each other with hardly a nod as their departure times raced to meet them.

Drivers disappeared into the black pit between the bogies, flare lamp and feeder in hand. Others bent alongside trimming corks with razor-sharp knives to fit the oiling points. Engines pulled up to water columns, sweat-soaked firemen clambered over coal and steel to drag the huge leather tube (the bag) into the tank. "OK" and the driver let go the torrent of water essential to fill a 4000 gallon tank in a few minutes.

Men searched for tools, collected sand from the hearth, trimmed head lamps, called on fitters, job on job. The noise and activity increased to bedlam, but a satisfying, delicious, exciting bedlam where each man knowing his job, cut his way through the noise and confusion to have that locomotive off the shed on time despite it all.

It was a magnificent feat of organisation and personal effort, carried out in a matter of fact, preoccupied sort of way by men who never thought it at all unusual. It happened every morning that came and went. To walk into it as a stranger would, I'm sure confuse, if not terrify. But to those who took part it was a stimulating, satisfying and unforgettable experience.

My thoughts now turned to the men who had guided me through my early years. It was long before steam had reached its' zenith that onto the footplate came these men who would, in time, command the greatest steam engines in the world. These men trod the footplate of Churchwood and Collett's mighty locos during the 1920's and 30's heading some of the most famous and fastest express trains that steam would ever produce. These men with whom I worked and knew so well had been part of this Great Western at its greatest.

I was privileged to join them when that great time was past, but the giant steam didn't die, or even become sick, overnight. It was as if he had passed his best while helping the country he served to defeat its enemies. Now he stood, proud and battered, unaware for the present of the weakness which would gradually force him to give way to different and even more powerful giants.

For years he went on as if it would all be the same again one day. It was not to be, but before the great giant of steam went on to rest he was capable of enormous feats of strength and skill. Like a great man past his best he could, and did, turn it on when needed. Turn it on he did, as he helped his stricken country drag itself from the sickness of war and to help its people to enjoy the fruits of peace as they never had before.

The soldiers had to come home. Thousands, no, what am I saying, millions of people were to see the cliffs and beaches that surround our lovely island, many of them for the first time. Homes had to be repaired and new ones built. Millions were to have homes of their own, secure jobs, holidays, plenty of food and a better life than ever before, and he had to provide transport on a massive scale.

What's more, he had to do it while healing his own wounds and repairing the damage and neglect of six years of conflict. It was during this conflict and its aftermath that I was to play my tiny part in his last revival. I was proud to join with the men who saw him at his best and to be there on many, many days when the old magic shone through.

When I walked away, the death throes of steam were years off, and glad I am not to have seen them.

CLEANING

I had my dearest wish at last. I was finally starting work as an Engine Cleaner at Oxley Shed. It was only by becoming an engine cleaner that it was possible to become a Locomotive fireman and eventually a driver. On the way down Jones Rd I had met two other first day cleaners and together we made our way through the wicket gate and left under Oxley viaduct to climb the steep curving path for the first time. It was winter, and barely light. We stopped, breathless at the brow of the embankment on the north side of the viaduct. In front of us was the foot crossing over the rails where they fan out into the many railroads which run down to Oxley Shed. We crossed over and followed the path down to the shed, passing the coal stage on the way. As we approached the red-brick shed buildings, smoke was billowing from under the arch of the massive doorway. This was created by an engine standing with its' belching chimney just inside the doors.

But our concern was with the door on our right which led to the lobby of the shed office. The booking area with its' rosters which listed the jobs at the station, departure times, names of the crews etc. This was itself a place of character. There was a sweet smell of old timber which, mixed with the acrid smell of coal and smoke, was surprisingly not unpleasant. It had many lockers; some of which had wide wooden surfaces, shining and worn by a thousand tired bottoms and elbows shuffling along as they waited for mates or filled in tickets.

The clerk in the time office listened slightly impatiently as I explained that we were new there. He gave us our checks (a round metal disk about the size of a 10p) and told us to return them when we booked off.

"See Charlie in the cleaners' cabin," he said, "he'll show you the way" pointing to a lad in black overalls and a face to match.

This lad, who looked like he'd been up and down somebody's chimney for years without a wash, walked out of the lobby with a toss of his filthy head which obviously meant 'Follow Me!' Now at fourteen years of age we were still at that age when getting dirty had a manly and quite desirable flavour of grown-up-ness about it but the state of this lad as we followed him into the growing daylight was a bit much for me.

His cap was covered in thick black grease, which I was later to discover came from scraping the bottom of the boiler while struggling about in the inside motion of an engine. His hair which was visible from the back seemed to be saturated in oil, his face and hands were completely black, but worst of all, a thick gob of dark grey grease, not unlike seagull droppings, was stuck to the back of his neck. As we followed him into the shed the atmosphere took our breath away; the noise of the engine blowers and the banging of fire irons from the engine on the going-out road, the thick, acrid smell of steam and smoke, but above all in the gaslit gloom dozens of massive locos of every type and size in all stages of readiness and unreadiness stood towering above us, the lines of them disappearing into the distant gloom.

I stood trying to take it all in but the lad leading us was nonchalant and slightly bored with it all. Such was his casual control of the situation that we already regarded him as a person of long experience in the depot. Imagine our surprise when we discovered later that he had been employed there for barely a fortnight.

"Come effing on," he shouted, "I'll take ya to see effing Charlie in the effing cabin. You'll see plenty of these effing engines before the day's out, I can effing tell ya.

"Well this was shock number two for although I was well acquainted with all the naughty words, I had never heard them used on such a scale before. I was soon to discover though, that his filthy state and his filthy mouth were not at all uncommon around Oxley Shed.

He led us past the stores window to a large wooden door in the corner of the shed, kicked it open and marched in.

A voice said, "Where do you think you've been, m'lad?" obviously referring to 'dirty-neck'. 'Dirty-neck' ignored the question and said in reply,

"These kids are startin' ere this mornin', must be effing mad". At that he walked right by Charlie (for Charlie it was) and sauntered down the cabin. Charlie was flustered. In order to deal with us, he had to let 'dirty-neck' go by.

"I'll see you later," he said as 'dirty-neck' walked towards the enormous fire roaring away at the far end of the long room.

Most surprising to us was the fact that he was rejoining about a dozen or so other lads all in the same filthy state. They were all different sizes and I found later (when washed) different in every way; but at the moment I first clapped eyes on them, they were all equally dirty and by the sound of things, equally foul-mouthed for 'f-ings' and 'b-ings' were bandied about enough to deafen us all.

Charlie shouted for silence several times, each time the noise level dropped a few decibels. Then with the arguments and swearing temporarily subdued, Charlie turned his attention to us. I was dazed by it all and wondered how he had the nerve to turn his back on such a wild mob. How could I imagine for one moment that in one week my fellow novices and I would have joined them; would be just as filthy as they were and almost as argumentative and foul-mouthed as they were (this takes a bit of practice) and seeing Charlie not as a protector and controller of the mob, but as the enemy, to be watched carefully, avoided and aggravated at every opportunity.

Poor old Charlie, no wonder he looked harassed and hurt, he had every right to be. He was a short, tubby man with a thick-set neck and a large head which was almost always crowned by a flat cap. A clean and fair, but serious sort of chap, not very fierce to look at but pretty tough nevertheless. His great downfall was his serious outlook on life. His charges consisted of between twelve and twenty young chaps aged from under 15 to about 17 years of age, all of them in a highly excitable state, due mainly to their youth of course, but aggravated by the fact that the nation was at war.

If you were not around at that time, then imagine a town thronged with soldiers from every corner of the globe. The Germans looking across the channel only 21 miles away and popping over now and again to drop a few bombs. There was talk of invasion, Parachute troops, spies, fighting in the streets, and so on and so on. In this turbulent, unsettled atmosphere imagine Charlie trying to get this shower interested in cleaning engines, the toilets, their own rest-room, or anything really, he had no chance!

To get back to the proceedings, standing at his large wooden desk Charlie was now taking down particulars of his latest recruits.

My father was a Senior Fireman at Oxley, his brother was a young driver and another brother was a firedropper at Stafford Rd, so I had all the right family connections. Charlie knew them all and after remarking how well-liked and regarded all my relations were, he took a long look at me then turned away without enthusiasm. He now tried once more to get control of the mob.

"Quiet!" he shouted. The noise level dropped a little more but otherwise they appeared to take no notice whatsoever. Charlie looked really frustrated and amazed at such disrespect (a state of mind that he seemed to be in most of the time I knew him).

"Shut your rotten faces!" he bellowed in a voice that must have reached most of the shed. The rotten faces turned towards us, resentful and rebellious but almost silent at last.

Charlie now addressed them again. "Come on, let's be having yer. That Tanky needs cleaning before one o'clock and it won't do itself, will it." For almost a minute the mob ignored this request, going silent and lethargic. Just as I had decided that they'd all been struck deaf and dumb, one or two of the weaker characters started to shuffle towards us reluctantly. These were followed, one by one, by the rest of the mob until they all assembled round us like a crowd of workhouse lads. I had ample opportunity now to observe the greasy hands and faces, the ripped and mucky overalls.

These were officially 'Engine Cleaners'. From their appearance, a stranger might conclude that they were used to clean the engines with! Ernie (the other charge-hand) was often heard to remark, "How you dozy B's get so bloody filthy without removing any muck from these engines is a soddin' mystery to me!"

Anyway, they all began to collect their equipment. This consisted of scrapers, skilly-cans, paraffin lamps, and most important of all, two large red signs demanding "DO NOT MOVE". These were supposed to be fixed to the lamp brackets of any engines worked, because to move an engine with someone 'underneath' would very likely result in a death or serious injury. It may seem unbelievable to you, as it does to me now, but we regarded the fixing of these plates as a bit of silly officialdom.

We frequently went underneath without them, the general feeling was that like cleaning your boots it was time wasting and no amount of stories about men crushed to death had any real impact. I think we regarded them as scare-mongering; done mainly to back up their peculiar officious ideas.

The mob now started to file out. "Just hang on here a minute," said Charlie as he followed them. We followed too, but only to stand in the corner of the shed watching Charlie trying to assert his authority over his underlings. It looked a pretty hopeless task to us, with each and every one of them apparently devoid of their senses. There seemed to be an unspoken pact that Charlie should be aggravated at every opportunity. With a dozen or so on to one, they were very very successful.

Each one of these greasy 'Wonacks' held a flare lamp of the type Aladdin was famous for. These consisted of a vessel with a spout, from the vessel through the spout was a chunky wick about one inch thick. Paraffin was poured into the vessel, the protruding wick was lit to give a flame and if that wasn't primitive I don't know what was. Naturally these objects came in for a lot of rough treatment and the wicks were often trapped in the spout. In such cases, the wick would become shorter and the flame with it, until the worse ones would give a piddling gleam of light that was neither use nor ornament.

On the other hand, a new one had a nice wad of wick sticking out and would give a six or eight inch flame. These in the hands of a greasy idiot could be coaxed into a flame as much as 18 inches in height, which would create a major fire hazard and almost as much smoke and pollution as a moderate-sized factory chimney. Mind you, in those days we had never heard of pollution. I don't think it was invented until after I had left the railway.

Can you imagine the scene, the great shed with its two massive turn-tables and all around the ghostly shapes of locomotives. All of them patchily lit by the lofty gas lamps. There was an engine on the middle road, between the two tables, and two more on the 'Going Out' roads known as the "Hearth" and "The Racecourse". This was because that side of the shed over-looked Dunstall Park Racecourse.

These three engines were surrounded by noise and activity, the bright light from the cabs and steam rising from the damped down coal indicated that they were almost ready for duty. All the remaining engines stood cold and lifeless, the term 'Dead' which was always applied to engines out of steam was somehow most appropriate.

On our side of the shed was the 51 Class Side Tanky which Charlie was trying to get the mob interested in. Some of them carried skilly cans and some a large wad of cotton waste but every one of them held a flare lamp. Some of these lamps were little better than the end of a lighted cigar; others flared away like a fire in a candle factory. They were held aloft as these lads went clambering over and under the Tanky; laughing, shouting arguing and none listening to Charlie. This pantomime was our introduction to the art of engine cleaning.

Amazing though it was, it seemed to work to a limited degree with each greasy 'twat' going to a different part of the engine and getting to work with varying degrees of enthusiasm. The general idea was, as far as I ever discovered, first to scrape off the thickest of the cheesy black muck then to stir a quantity of skilly into the remaining filth with a well soaked gob of cotton waste. When this was done the resultant gunge would be wiped off with a clean piece of waste and the process repeated until, to the mild surprise of everyone, clean bright metal would often be revealed. Similar treatment was sometimes given to the painted parts of the loco but usually such cleaning as we did was confined to the working parts of the engine in order that the preparing driver could clamber about without getting completely filthy and even see the places he was supposed to oil.

As most cleaners were engaged on pit cleaning, coaling, ash loading and other labouring jobs, the cleaning of engines was very restricted indeed. However, when cleaning work was needed, it should have been obvious to any sensible person, that the best method was to clean as many parts properly in the time that you had available. As I recall, we seemed to have great difficulty in understanding this simple fact.

Consequently it was not uncommon for an engine to be seen leaving the shed with one side quite immaculate and the other filthy. And who can know the indignation of a young cleaner who, having spent all his time on one beautifully clean, nay, gleaming connecting rod, on an otherwise filthy loco, receives from Charlie instead of expected gasps of admiration, a thorough tongue lashing for the stupid sod he was. But as Ernie (the other charge-hand) often remarked, "If any of us possessed either common-sense or a sense of proportion, then we certainly didn't bring them to work with us."

Well by now Charlie had imparted some idea of his intentions to the mob and was now returning to us with the sort of hang-dog look of a man who has just fallen into the canal whilst escaping from his burning house. We followed him back into the cabin to see that two of the greasy monkeys were still in there. They were sitting with their unmentionable boots on the table and talking a load of nonsensical rubbish. Charlie soon put a stop to all that.

"You two can take these three new 'uns to clean the lavs," he said. The most aggressive of the two jumped to his feet with a look of utter outrage. "Aye, arf a mo Charl," he shouted, "we did 'em last wick. It's somebody else's turn this wick."

"Well I don't think you did do 'em last wick," replied Charlie quick as a flash, "But if you did do 'em last wick, you're doin' em agen this wick." Neither lad seemed in any way satisfied with this but Charlie completely ignored their muttering and moaning and gave his orders.

Accordingly, we grabbed hold of several galvanised metal buckets, then walked over to the Bosh to fill them with hot water. On our return Charlie ladled some extremely unpleasant looking soft soap and a dash of disinfectant into each bucket. We then walked along to the toilets to the chorus of 'Here come the sh..house cleaners' from the mob. We pushed the toilet door open to see a long urinal on the wall on our right, the far wall had an arched opening about two feet from the floor; through this the cold morning light struck along the blue bricks. On our left there was a short passage with four WC compartments on each side. The doors of these were cut so short that the legs and boots of each user was on view for all to see. I was surprised to see this and a little disturbed, after all, who doesn't value a bit of privacy on such occasions. I was to find later that this was one of the most modern of all shed toilets including Stafford Rd, none of the cubicles of which had (or ever had) any doors at all! Anyway, the idea was to clean the pans with the brush provided, then clean and swill down the walls and floor as required.

As it transpired, Charlie seemed to do most of the work himself because the two Old Hands went even more dense than they were when cleaning engines. It was obvious that they considered cleaning the lav's way below their notice, even rookies like us had little interest in 'bog cleaning'. Nevertheless we did enjoy the hosing down and the vigorous sweeping. The warm, soapy smell laced with disinfectant, mingled with the sooty, oily smell of the shed to give an exciting and unique flavour even to this lowly job. By the time the loo's were cleaned, the daylight was penetrating the odd corners of the shed and it was time for a little lunch.

The three of us had lunch on our own, being on day shift and then went out to assist the other two lads who were cleaning the engine pits. The first hour or so of this consisted mainly of dodging around engines and in and out of pits whilst throwing filthy gobs of oily waste at each other. I soon found that a large, soaking, oily patch up the lug-hole sharpened one's reflexes no end, and encouraged one to join the game. Was it for this then that I'd washed me hair, polished me boots 'til they'd shone and donned me brand new overalls.

Charlie appeared from nowhere whilst this tom-foolery was in progress and said how disappointed he was to see me involved in such games, then separated us putting me with one of the old hands to clean the pit by the sand hearth. We took it in turns to shovel and barrow the ashes to the top door where the ash wagon always stood. The wheel barrow was of all metal construction, including the wheel, and it deserved a prize as the worst designed wheel barrow of all time. It weighed more empty than most barrows did full, and the handles were so far apart that only a giant of a man could feel at home with one. As I was a 9 and a 1/2 stone streak of a lad, these barrows were agony. It soon became a competition between the loader and the wheeler to see if the first could load more than the second could wheel. It was then decided that to put the barrow down before the ash wagon was reached was a sign of weakness. The result of this stupidity was that the last few yards were absolute agony. Just before you tipped the wheel barrow,a pain developed between the shoulder-blades which felt like being torn apart. Of course such suffering demanded a long rest between trips so that only a modest amount of real work was done. The only consolation was in the evil fun you could have, watching your mate struggling and wobbling his painful way to the ash wagon.

It was my turn to shovel and my mate had just started on his distressing run to the wagon when a rough-looking character sauntered over from the direction of the sand hearth.

"Aye kid," he said, spitting onto the blue bricks, "How'd ya like to do me a favour?"

10

I was out of the pit in a flash, nodding my head off and proving how green I really was.

"Tek that barra of ashes up the tip will yer" he asked. I was off like a shot. The barrow was loaded up to the hilt with wet ashes. Arms at full stretch, a pain like a knife wound between the shoulder blades. The barrow was tipped and on my return the hearth man was ready with a shovel for me to load a second one. Coming back with this trip I met Charlie.

"What do ya think you're doing Browny?" he inquired.

"I'm helping the man in the sand hearth" I replied, expecting at least a nod of approval.

"Help him?" asked Charlie, aghast. "Help him? He can help his ruddy self he can, he's had you for a proper mug, he has. You must be going soft. Anyway, get down to the cabin. It's dinner time." I was flabbergasted. In a couple of hours I'd upset Charlie twice and all while trying to do my best.

We had our dinner and soon after, the afternoon shift came on at which time Charlie instructed two of them to take us newcomers to 'do' the sand hearth. I was pleased as punch to have a different job to do. The sand hearth was big and quite as well built as many a church or chapel and it was entirely devoted to drying sand in readiness for the locomotive sanding gear.

We entered from the shed through a large, arched opening. Immediately inside was an area probably ten feet by twelve feet which somehow always seemed to resemble a large cave. On the left were the furnaces built into the steel frame of the sand hearth. On the right was the stationary engine and the rough shelter that was home to the men who worked there. We turned sharp left, walking single file past the sand bins where the firemen filled their buckets while preparing engines. At the far end a steel ladder gave access to the upper floor above the furnaces. Climbing over the top we found ourselves in an area perhaps twenty feet by twelve feet, completely covered with soft yellow sand. Our job, we discovered gradually, was to shovel the dry sand into the bins, then shovel the damp sand to the hottest place so that it would dry. Like almost everything I ever did while a cleaner at Oxley, it soon became a wild and boisterous competition. This started quite lethargically, then speeded up, ending, as it always did in a bout of wrestling, shouting and swearing that would have done justice to cage full of baboons.

One of the older hands was a bit of a know all, so when he began to get more than he bargained for he quickly brought it to an end with a fine show of self righteousness.

We then sat around in the warm sand, chatting. Everything was new to us and there was no end to our thirst for knowledge of railroads. Then young 'know-all' began a tale of his personal experiences whilst being bombed along the south coast. We found out later that this was largely fiction but it made an interesting story nevertheless. Then our attentions were directed to the sand wagon. On the side of the Hearth opposite the shed were a number of arched openings which looked out onto a single track and standing on it was the sand wagon. We first jumped into the wagon then competed to see who could throw a shovel full of sand through the opening and farthest across the hearth. At no time did it occur to us to see who could throw the most sand in, oh dear no!

It seemed no time at all before someone said it was time to go for a wash at which we all raced across to the bosh where we spent fifteen minutes or so trying to soak or scald each other, somehow washing a little muck off in the process.

Although we novices had done nothing to get really dirty, nevertheless we were! So at the appointed time we returned our checks to the booking office, sporting black rings around our eyes, black around our noses and filling our ears. So ended my first day at Oxley. I don't think the railways had profited much, but I'd enjoyed myself enormously

THE WEDNESBURY SHUNTER

The Wednesbury South End shunter could be a busy job especially on nights. It was an exchange siding between the LMS, (later the London Midland Region of British rail) and the Great Western, (Later the Western Region). The LMS line ran under the Great Western so that the exchange siding were many feet below our sidings. The LMS shunters would put out vans and waggons destined for us, while our shunters would do the opposite. The route down to the exchange sidings which for some reason was known as 'The Farm', was very steep and rickety.

Whether it was because of joint ownership I never did know, but 'The Farm' was about the roughest area of sidings that I ever saw. The lower you went, the worse it got. The rails seemed to have many kinks in them and at numerous points the sleepers were on soft ground or occasionally, on no ground at all, so that when moving, the engine seemed to be going up and down and sort of shuffling about in an alarming fashion.

To watch these pannier tankys coming up of 'The Farm' from a distance was fascinating. They gave the impression of moving in all directions at once.

The main task of the South End shunting engine was to bring large rafts of waggons up off 'The Farm' and then shunt them on the comparatively level yard of the Great Western. Each raft would be pulled up the bank and over the points to be shunted back in the same direction. There were several reasons, (which I shall not bore you with) why it was frequently convenient to pull off 'The Farm' with those extra few waggons. Now, as it was normal to pull off with a very long and heavy 'rafts' of waggons anyway, you can imagine that it was quite the normal thing for us to start pulling with only the sketchiest idea of whether or not, we should get over the top. In fact, it was not uncommon for the engine to come to a stand and have to go back down, either for another run, or to hook a few off.

The consequence of all this was that the shunter, particularly on nights, could be very entertaining. The routine was, the shunter would walk up and shout, "Right, were going down The Farm to pick a raft up". He would then jump on the step and ride down the bank with the engine bucking up and down and shuffling right and left as we went. The fireman would put the blower on and smack some coal round her in readiness for the pull back. When we reached the waggons the shunter would disappear, sometimes for quite a long time.

When he reappeared he would climb up on to the footplate and have a quick debate with the driver about the number of waggons he was hoping we could pull off. The driver would normally agree as the shunters had a far better idea of what an engine could pull off 'The Farm' than the loco men did. The snag was though, no one could be absolutely sure because the waggons and contents could vary wildly in weight from time to time.

By this time the fireman had usually got the engine blowing of steam through the safety valve with a noise which could certainly be heard 5 miles away. The driver would open the regulator and the sand lever and once the couplings were tight he would push the regulator right across the guide.

Despite the sand the tanky would usually slip a time or two as she struggled to raise speed. Each slip would add to the horrendous noise as the engine exhaust roared and rattled away. In addition to the noise, the exhaust would be sending a massive column of steam and sparks, like an enormous roman candle, high into the night sky.

These engines were extremely strong and had incredible acceleration up to about 40 mph so within seconds the exhaust would be roaring like a lion as the speed increased. As the bank got steeper, the engine would begin to slow down again and it was frequently touch and go whether we should get them over the bank or not. At the height of the speed and commotion the noise was enough to wake the whole of Wednesbury.

Usually, we would just make it and the engine would begin to pick up speed again and stop bucking about as we reached the Great Western sidings. Now we had to shunt these waggons into the correct order for the various trains which would leave later. The method of doing this was to run toward the siding at speed as the shunter hooked each group of waggons off. We would then apply the brake and reverse the lever to go back without stopping. The free waggons would go racing up the yard for the under shunter to slow them down and hook them onto the appropriate train.

This usually involved the engine running back and forth with the roar of the exhaust alternating with the screeching of the brakes for half the night. It could be quite exciting and stimulating at times, and it was hardly ever dull, but now when I think of the black smoke and rocketing columns of sparks, plus the incredible noise that ensured for a great deal of the night, all within a few yards of several rows of houses, I wonder how the hell they got any sleep at all.

At the time I cannot recall giving it much thought. It was absolutely amazing how much noise and pollution those people were prepared to put up with, with only occasional protests.

This process, of running forward while the Head Shunter hooked off. Then stopping at his signal to pull back again was carried to it's ultimate at Oxley North sidings. Oxley North sidings sloped steeply up hill from the shunting spur to the many splayed out roads which formed the sidings. Because of the fairly steep incline it was necessary to run forward at some speed, or 'hit em up' as it was always known.

The method was for the shunter to hook those waggons off which were intended for any one road, he would then call the engine forward with hand signals, or his lamp at night, often shouting "Hit em up!" at the same time. At this the driver would push the regulator right across the guide to accelerate as fast as possible. The Head shunter would judge when the speed was high enough for the several waggons to reach those they were intended to be joined with, at which point, he would order the engine to stop and go back.

On this order the driver would smack the steam brake full on and reverse the engine on the move. He would then open the regulator wide again to regain his starting position as quick as possible to start the whole thing over again.

At each run the Under Shunter would be waiting for each group of waggons and as they approached the train they were destined for he would control the speed by applying the waggon brakes with his shunting pole and finally hooking them on. This was a very dangerous job requiring a great deal of running about across sleepers and rails while concentrating totally on where and how fast the waggons were coming. The shunter was, in effect playing a massive game of chess. Both he and the under-shunter had to be very alert, and very very fit.

On the engine it was one continuous repetition of forward acceleration, followed by braking and backward acceleration and so on. This could go on for hours and was most often shared between the driver and the fireman. I have spent quite a few stimulating nights doing this work, and I can testify that it kept you well awake and occupied you totally. On the night shift the roman candle effect from the chimney which the rapid acceleration produced was almost continuous. It was quite exciting for a young fireman to find himself performing this energetic and important work so early in his career. It was stimulating, exciting and vital work.

I don't think that anyone who did it could ever quite forget it.

THE BISCUIT

I was a fireman by now and it was the most difficult stage of the second world war. Food had long become a problem and it was particularly so for men who worked unpredictable shifts like footplate men. Things got so bad at one time that canteens were opened at most major sheds or stations. Although the food was spartan and thinly spread it did provide some small extras if you were working longer than you had bargained for. As time went by these canteens acquired little extras like Biscuits or the odd cake or two. Such an occasion had occurred at Oxley and the biscuits were not the normal round or finger biscuits but large thick biscuits of a type which had not been seen by us for quite a few years.

The formidable canteen manageress decided that these biscuits would be restricted to one per person. Now you may think one biscuit was hardly worth bothering with, but with almost every item of food rationed and the rest in short supply a biscuit of this type and quality took on an importance which it is difficult to explain in this world which overflows with good food. When the large tins were opened, greedy eyes stared across the counter as one of the canteen assistants ripped the paper covering to reveal this positive treasure trove of goodies.

No sooner had the ration of 1 per person been announced, the counter disappeared from view, hidden by a queue of men anxious to get their share. In no time at all they were returning to their seats with their biscuits held like prized possessions. Some would take them home to share with their spouse, some would take them home for their children and a few greedy sods would just sit and and wolf them down there and then. The Crew man in our crowd had been telling us about his two grandchildren and it was clear that they were the apples of his eye. When he returned to his seat with his biscuit he began to wrap it carefully in the remains of his food wrapping , saying as he did, "I shall have to make sure I divide that equally between them or I shall be in real trouble".
We needed no telling that he was referring to his grandchildren.

After a while all the immediate occupants of the canteen had been served and, like a gale force wind, the massage had passed, to every railway man within walking distance. Soon, they too had been in and had their biscuits. When all the immediate customers had been served, there were still a couple of tins of biscuits unopened.

Then it started, so innocently, some Bright Herbert leaned over to Crewe man and suggested, "Why don't you get another biscuit, your grand kids will have one each then".

Crewe man looked shocked, "Oh no, I couldn't do that, those are for people who havn't had one yet", he replied shaking his head.

"Go on", urged Bright Herbert, "There has been so many men through that queue by now they will have forgotten us completely, I bet we could all go and get another without them noticing".

Crewe man was still shaking his head but it was clear that he could already see the delight on two young faces as he turned up with one each of these quite unusual and massive biscuits.

Another of our crowd bent over and said in a low but urgent voice,

"Go on, get one, they wont know and we wont say anything, one biscuit aint much between two healthy kids, they're entitled to a bit of a treat".

Crew man was still doubtful but now several low voices were urging him to do this dastardly thing and obtain another biscuit by deception. Slowly the idea was growing on Crew man and finally and still reluctantly he rose to his feet.

"Just walk up as if you've just come in", said one.

"For Gods sake, you aint stealing the crown jewels", said another in exasperation.

Crewe man rose like a man in a dream, nodding to all his accomplices. He walked to the counter and joined the short queue which waited for the cup of tea or the odd slice of toast, but none for biscuits.

By this time the ridiculous humour of the situation had become apparent and several of his erstwhile accomplices were now finding it almost impossible not to collapses with laughter as Crewe man stood like a condemned man awaiting his fate. Eventually, after what seemed an age, his turn came, "Can I have a cup of tea and one of those biscuits please", he said in a voice which had gone high and reedy.

"Yes luv", the canteen assistant replied without hesitation. She turned to get his tea and said to the older lady who stood back a little, "Get him his biscuit Hilda, will you please".

Hilda walked over to the unopened biscuit tin and reached in for one of these objects of great delight and walked over to present Crewe man with it.

As she reached the counter she stopped with the biscuit poised and stared suspiciously, "Ere, you havn't had one before have you", she asked

Crewe man turned the colour of a freshly boiled beetroot and his voice dried up completely, he was clearly not the man to join the secret service or anything like that.

Watching all this was the manageress herself, she was cutting a loaf, she walked swiftly over to where Crewe man stood having the worst moments of his entire life and said in a loud, stentorian voice, "You have had one already havn't you, you blackguard".
Then pointing the knife in a most threatening manner she shouted, "Come on admit it you have had one".

Crewe man nodded his head in confusion, he would clearly have given all he had to be fifty miles from Oxley canteen at that moment. The first woman was saying something about it being people like him who are losing the war for us.

At this ridiculous statement all the blokes in our crowd collapsed into gales of laughter. Some helpful whatsit shouted, "Have him shot missis, his mother's a German". In no time at all the women were condemning the whole lot of us as brigands and traitors, if not worse and Crewe man looked as if he was about to be hanged. We all wisely left the canteen at this point and as we walked up the bank we explained to Crewe man how ridiculous it was for grown women to make such a fuss over just one biscuit.

Crewe man was not impressed and made it clear that he suspected that we had done it all deliberately. I bet he remembered that night till the end of his days and I'm damned sure he never saw the inside of Oxley canteen again.

BIG JOHN

Big John appeared at the door of the Oxley canteen. In the last few hours he'd taken aboard enough canteen ale to leave many men paralytic. John was not paralytic, but he did have a visible wobble with each step. Accompanying him were four firemen whose ages ranged from 17 to 19. The whole company were in their best togs, for it was Friday, pay day, they had all collected their money. Then they had adjourned to the canteen for a game of cards, a yarn, a laugh and of course, some ale. The firemen were all well dressed according to the fashion of the times but none could compare with Big John. He was a driver, and old enough to be the father of his companions. Nevertheless, he was a smart and handsome figure. His six foot three, well-proportioned frame looked well in an elegantly cut suit. His dark overcoat was set off by a long silk scarf trailing beside its open edges. His final crowning glory though, was an immaculate Homburg hat.

Yes, when he was dressed up, our John could pass as a peer of the realm, always providing of course, that he kept his mouth shut. John was about to do what he usually did when the pubs were shut and there was nowt else to do. He was going home, but first he had to complete, as all drinking men do, the conversation that he had started inside. Big John had been giving these young and single hopefuls some inside tips on the more delicate features of making love. Now, contrary to what you might have been led to believe whilst listening to them boasting in the cabin, these four young blades had little real knowledge of this most engaging subject, and even less experience.

Consequently, they were all ears. John was holding forth on all the intimate details of the bedroom in a most explicit manner, which in those days, was no less than sensational. His theories had a straight forward, simplistic style that appealed instantly to his audience. These young men were most impressed and only too ready to give John's methods a try at the first opportunity, but to be honest, they had more chance of flying over the viaduct on the way home. Still, it gave them something to dream about in their lonely beds.

Just then, walking down the bank came Charlie and his mate. Charlie wore a tightly-belted mac which had a slightly military air about it. His railway cap was worn at just the right angle and together with his large gauntlet gloves and bicycle clips, he looked a proper little action man. His mate on the other hand, had the air of a man suffering the effects of the night before. He walked with a weary step and couldn't wait to collapse into Charlie's side-car to be whisked home.

The motorbike and the side-car were parked just a yard or so from where Big John was holding audience. Charlie nodded to John as he wheeled his bike onto the path.

He lived quite near to John and naturally said, "Want a lift home, John?"

'Arr, I don't mind," replied John quickly; he was not too keen on waiting for the bus. Somehow his imposing figure didn't quite fit into a bus queue and he was always glad to avoid it.

He walked over to Charlie and the bike, without as much as a word of 'Good-bye' to his young companions. They began to disperse awkwardly. For all the attention that John now paid them, they might well have been invisible.

"How about if I have a go", said John suddenly, referring to the driving of Charlie's machine, of course. "I ain't rode one of these things for years", he went on, for all the world as if this was a perfect reason for doing so. Now of 300 odd drivers at Wolverhampton depot, I only knew one who would have let Big John near a vehicle of theirs in his present state. It was Charlie's misfortune to be that one.

Mind you, even Charlie, adventurous and cavalier though he could be, was taken aback by the thought of a drunken Big John driving them home. He was trying to think of an acceptable excuse for refusing. His fireman, young and lowly as he was, had no such inhibitions.

"Doh lerrim do it, Charlie," he shouted, "He's blind drunk, he'll kill us all!", Big John just chuckled and put it down to the young fellow's nervousness.

Before Charlie had time to think, John was astride the machine. "Get on Charl", he shouted, and 'Charl' climbed on the pillion. He was now looking over John's shoulder, trying to give him a quick refresher on the control of a motorbike. John was hardly listening. He kicked the bike into life and it leapt forward only to stall and stop again. He did this another twice, giving his passengers a thorough shaking in the process. As he kicked the engine into life for the fourth time. The fireman began to struggle to his feet.

"I'm getting out!" he shouted in a panic. But he had left it too late.

In later years, Charlie must have said a thousand times how astonished he was that he was able to hang onto Big John's overcoat. Because by all accounts, they left the railway path at about sixty miles an hour, went under the viaduct, up Jones' Rd and left into South St in a flash of light. It hardly seems possible that Big John could have changed direction four times in such a short distance at a really high speed. It may be that Charlie in his confused and terrified state could have exaggerated the speed a trifle. Nevertheless, we can rely on it that they were going at quite a lick.

Big John had found the throttle without much trouble but he seemed to have no idea where the brake was. South St passed in a blur and they shot out into Stafford Rd in one sweep; they not only failed to stop at the Halt sign, they nearly took it with them. They were now roaring along the middle line of Stafford Rd. Charlie was pleading, at the top of his voice, for his drunken tormentor to slow down, but his words were torn from his lips in John's slipstream. The bike hurtled roughly towards the entrance of Bushbury Lane.

Just then a double-decker bus appeared and pushed out a little into Stafford Rd, exactly where John was planning to drive. This threw John for a moment and he straightened up and carried on. Just as Charlie was convinced that they were going up Oxley Bank on the wrong side of the road and into the face of oncoming traffic, John turned. He did so at right-angles causing the sidecar with it's terrified occupant to leave the ground. Then they hurtled into the most mind-blowing seconds of the whole trip!

Dividing the Croft car park from the pavement were a row of unyielding concrete posts and on the curb side was a cast iron pole. Charlie had previously thought the pavement between these two obstacles barely wide enough for pedestrians. Big John was now about to prove that it was ample for a motorbike and sidecar at high speed. In a moment of sheer terror they passed through with inches to spare.

Only a few yards beyond this point was the bus stop. I'm sure that every one of a dozen or so folk in that bus queue relived the fear and astonishment of that moment many times. We can easily imagine their state of mind as they saw Big John and his two open-mouthed and petrified passengers bombing along the pavement in a cloud of dust and a roar of exhaust.

If John had not managed to regain the road before they reached that queue, this tale would have had a dramatic and very sad end; but he did manage it so the bike tore on up Bushbury Lane like a scalded cat. Charlie was now making fresh attempts to get John to stop. He was hoarse from shouting into the cold wind. But John was deaf to all such panicky rubbish. The next hazard was a parked bus. It stood near that left-hand turn with the old chapel on the corner. To overtake it seemed a simple task until Charlie spotted a car coming in the opposite direction.

Now, as a motorbike rider, Charlie was no chicken, I can personally testify to that. In fact he had been called a 'Wild Swine' many times. Even so, Charlie assured me that even a madman would have stopped and let that car come through, and I believed him. Not so John. He decided to accelerate out of trouble. Even Charlie was astonished by the acceleration of his old bike. They took off like an 'Isle of Man' job. Well, they did get through, but only by a coat of varnish, and only because the terrified car driver stood hard on a very good set of brakes. Once again, Big John had made the day memorable for someone by revealing the Angel of Death approaching at great speed.

As they passed by the Oxley Arms and started up the incline of the bridge, things seemed remarkably normal. The gradient was slowing them down to about twice the legal limit. Charlie tried once again to appeal to John's commonsense, as if he had any. As they approached the hump of the bridge John seemed to hear Charlie's voice for the first time and with the single-mindedness of the blind drunk he half turned round to shout "What ya on about, Charl?" Charl nearly died as John veered over the crown of the road straight towards a lorry. Charlie shrieked in John's lughole and pushed him back to look forward in an attempt to avoid a collision. John over-reacted and for the second time in a few minutes they mounted the pavement. As John struggled to gain control, they careered down the pavement with the sidecar scraping the wall. Walking up the bridge towards them was a bent and weary figure in overalls. He was clearly a Bushbury 'Shed man', just popped out at the end of his shift to buy a packet of fags.

He was shuffling along with the slow and weary step of a man longing for his bed. One look at Big John on the thundering death machine and the weariness fell from him like a cloak. Luckily for him, he was near the gate which led to Bushbury sheds and with an almost miraculous burst of energy he disappeared through that opening like a rabbit down a hole.

Back on the road again, John shouted over his shoulder, "I think I'm getting the hang of this now."

"Thank God for that then," screamed Charlie from the bottom of his heart.

The rest of the trip was uneventful, John did overtake a bloke on a bike just as he was indicating a right turn into Sixteenth Avenue, but that was six of one and half a dozen of the other. The bloke shouted, "Idiot!" at John, and John bellowed back, "Imbecile!", in a voice that left Charlie deaf in one ear.

Otherwise the trip was uneventful and they pulled onto the front of the Butlers Arms, coming to a stand in three jumps and stops which shook the passengers to the core. Finally the stalled engine fell silent and the two reluctant passengers experienced the great peace that comes to those who have just had (as the Americans say) a life-threatening experience.

John climbed off the bike and wobbled gently as he surveyed the front of the 'Butlers Arms' with an affectionate eye. Then turning to Charlie he said "I quite enjoyed that, Charl."

"That's more than we bloody well did", replied Charl with great feeling. John patted Charlie affectionately on the back and said,

"You're a card you are, Charl. See ya" and with that he ambled off, totally unaware of the effects his drunken antics had had on his sober companions. He would hardly recalled these events in the morning, most of the terrifying images would have faded in the drunken haze and the night's sleep. But to his companions it remained a vivid and unforgettable memory, and an often told yarn that would stay with them to the end of their lives.

The fireman often laughed with near hysterics as he saw again the faces of the bus queue through the dust, and again as he recalled the astonishing change that came over the poor sod on the bridge. In fact, we should really give Charlie's mate the last word on this short drama. After all, didn't he face imminent death several times, up at the sharp end?

He climbed from the sidecar on shaky legs, his face still ashen, and said, "Charl, I always knew you were an idiot, but I never thought you would be daft enough to let a drunken bugger like that take us for a ride on your bike. It's a bloody miracle we're here to tell the tale".

With that, he walked away and as he left, Charlie could only agree with every word.

THE PARROT.

Such were the varied and unusual pursuits of the 500 odd men who peopled Stafford Rd and Oxley Sheds, that, no matter what you proposed to do there was always someone on hand who'd done it, been there, and could advise and encourage or discourage just as the fancy took them.

On this Sunday morning the shed was particularly still and quiet. In the corner of the locomen's cabin sat a pale and not too robust looking youth. Sitting across the table from him with his back turned to him and reading the news paper was his mate, a big fleshy man who we shall call Big Head. It was about a week earlier, whilst working the basin shunter that Pale Face had mentioned to Big Head that he was considering buying a parrot.

"A bloody parrot"! his over bearing mate had hooted, "What the hell do you want a bloody parrot for". Big Head could never see the point in anyone doing anything that he didn't want to do himself.

Pale face mumbled pathetically that he, "Loiked parrots", and anyway his best mates father had one.

"Well your best mates father might have a boil on his arse, it's no reason for you to want one is it"? Big head taunted.

In the face of Big Heads torrent of disparaging comments Pale Face had found it impossible to produce one truly adequate reason for buying a parrot, although he was becoming increasingly determined to own one if only to spite Big Head.

Eventually, Big head had ordered him, not asked, or suggested you understand, but ordered Pale Face not to think of buying a bloody parrot until he had had a word with Farmer Sid, because "Sid knew a thing or two about parrots, don't you bother".

Now, by good fortune, or so Big head had said, they were in the cabin and who should be sleeping the sleep of the just and knackered out, in that very cabin, but the Oracle of parrots, Farmer Sid himself. It was difficult to see this fount of all knowledge because the intervening table top mercifully obscured most of him, but his presence was evident by the gentle sawing sound of his breathing which confirmed that Sid was still alive. Every so often, a sudden throaty and alarming choking sound would interrupt the gentle snoring as Sid came near to swallowing his false teeth. Each time this happened Pale Face looked around in mild concern but Big Head continued to read his newspaper in total disregard.

After what seemed to Pale Face, a life time of waiting in the unusually quiet cabin, Sid began to move. Slowly the battered face of Sid came into view, the hat which was an almost permanent part of the face was missing. Some how, the the sparce and wispy hair gave the face a strangely comical appearance.

Farmer Sid's complexion had been described, by one who was a master of the spoken verb as "Like a bag of bosted plums". Before the head was barely upright, the searching hand had found the cap, rammed it on his head and the strange, formidable and familiar look of Sid returned.

He stared straight forward with the unseeing eyes of a man not yet ready to face the world. After a second or two of re-arranging his false teeth with his tongue, an activity which distorted his already alarming features still further, he then made a ceremony of spitting in the ashes surrounding the stove and stamping and snorting just to announce his return to the land of the living.

Big Head shook his paper, "Some tca in that can", He said without actual looking up.

Sid nodded, then with blank and mechanical slowness he poured himself a cup of hot, well stewed tea. As he sipped the tea Sid's face gradually came to life, his features gradually lost the puffiness of sleep and his eyes regained their normal light.

Big Head lowered his paper, "He wants to buy a bloody parrot Sid", he said loudly nodding towards Pale Face.

Sid turned his rather fierce, intimidating countenance full on Pale Face, "Yo want to buy a soddin parrot?" he shouted incredulously.

Pale Face nodded with as much composure as he could muster adding in a wavering voice, "I thought it ud be good loike".

"Good!" Sid exploded, "Good? , it's very good if you want something in your house as will make a noise fit to deafen an elephant whenever it feels like it, if that's what you want it is very, very good. And if you fancy something that is waiting to take the end off ya finger at the first opportunity, if that's what you're after a parrots wonderful. Oh, and if you want something that deposits four times it's own weight in manure in the bottom of it's sodding cage every hour of the day, if that's what your after you couldn't do better than a parrot. I'll tell you one thing you will spend all your time shovelling sh— as long as you've got a parrot".

There is little doubt that Sid had employed a degree of exaggeration. Never the less, with nary another word he arose to attend to one of those little jobs which must be done after sleeping all morning and then drinking tea.

Big Head looked insufferably self satisfied but said nothing.

Pale Face never did buy that parrot.

FRANK

Frank pushed his bike through the blackout doors with some difficulty and several disparaging comments laced with a naughty word or two. All of it said in a benign and good humoured way, because that was what he essentially was, benign and good humoured. Admitted, if you were on the the wrong end of one of his scathing and sarcastic attacks he would seem anything but.

"Hello mate", he said, spotting me at the notices, "How've ya slept".

"Oh, not too bad, thank ya Frank", I Replied, a bit relieved to hear such kindly concern after the tirade at the black out screens. Frank walked his bike to the wall of the small shed, leaned it carefully then walked back to where I stood. He first unbuttoned his overcoat, then lifted his food bag from around his neck and placed it more comfortably on his shoulder. He then stood filling his pipe and surveying the notice boards.

"Arr well, let's see what horrible things they've got in store for us tonight", he snorted between sucking and blowing at his pipe.

The notice boards stood in the entrance to the shed on the wall which hid the Foreman's office. Facing them was the booking office, the half glass wall of which threw light on to the notices. These notices were a focal point for all loco men, because the notices would show every job at Stafford Rd Loco Shed from the lowliest shunter to the crack expresses. Alongside the jobs appeared the names of the men who would be working each job on that day and the next.

As the time for the job drew near, those jobs requiring a steam engine would have the appropriate number written alongside. They were in chronological order from mid-night to mid-night each twenty four hours.

Our jobs were grouped into 'Links', a link being a group of jobs of similar importance, but having various times around the clock. Most men knew their mates in their own link, and usually those in links just a little higher or lower. The consequence was that these notices were the subject of great interest and speculation.

By studying these notices one could discover all manner of things about the men at the depot. Who was ill, who was on holiday, who had swopped shifts and so on and so on. A really skilled observer, and Frank had long been one of those, would know when someone was working a flanker in seconds.

However, all was well tonight and in minutes we were on our way, out into the blackness to report to the Zone supervisor at Oxley. Once there, we were given a job almost immediately, to relieve a train in the loop. It was a 28er with a small load of less than 25 waggons so the run to Tyseley would be simplicity itself. We ran with all the 'sticks' off through Bilston but were turned into the loop at Wednesbury. After a few minutes watching the loop signal, expecting it to come off any moment, the Guard climbed onto the footplate.

"We're not going from here for a while Frank", he informed us.

"Oh arr, what's up then", asked Frank.

"There's a derailment at Handsworth and it could take em till morning to clear it".

"Serious?" Frank asked.

"No, I don't think so, just someone doing a shunt and didn't go right over the points, we'll hear more a bit later on I expect.

Frank nodded thoughtfully, "Might as well make ourselves comfortable then".

It was a mild and pleasant night and the footplate was quite warm and cosy so it took only minutes with shovel and waste for Frank to make a more comfortable place to sit. I turned the bucket upside down in the corner and leaned against the overcoats. Instead of going back to his comfortable van the guard sat on the fireman's seat chatting for a while. He wanted to know how long a certain Driver had been on the railway. Knowing that this driver was about the same seniority as Frank he guessed that Frank would know. He wasn't wrong and Frank soon put him right.

The Guard seemed loath to leave, "How long have you been on the Footplate Frank", he asked.

"Too bloody long", Frank replied cagily.

"I reckon you was on the railway during the first World War wasn't ya Frank".

Arr, I was", Frank confirmed and pulled at his pipe in a way which I knew indicated that he was in the mood for a yarn.

"Were ya born in Wolverhampton Frank"?

"Tettenhall!", Frank replied loudly, in a tone which implied that Tettenhall was much better. Our family have been Tettenhall folk for years, I don't know how long but my Grandfather on my fathers side owned the Shoulder of Mutton in Wood Rd back in the 1800s, as early as 1870 I think".

"The Shoulder of Mutton"? the guard repeated a bit like a parrot, "I've been in there, it's a small place aye it Frank"?

"Arr, it is", Frank confirmed, "But me Grandfather made a living out of it for years, that and metal working that is".

"Metal working Frank", the Guard repeated.

Frank removed his pipe and looked hard at the him, "You any relation to a parrot mate".

The Guard ignored the insult he was clearly interested in Franks family history and so was I.   Frank went on, "Arr, he used to be what was known as a 'White Smith' as well as a Brewer, although me father brewed the beer for him in later years, when we was kids. It was a free house then of course, they owned it, beer was a penny a pint and a cheese sandwich thrown in. When they'd had two pints that was enough of that stuff so me grandfather would send em home with a free clay pipe".

"How did he come to do metal work in a place like Tettenhall Frank"?

"Oh there was a lot of metal workers round there in the last half of the 19th century, they used to do the work at the back of their houses and take it into Wolverhampton on the pony cart to one of the buyers and then bring orders for more work and the metal to do it with, back with them.   If there weren't no orders they would get blind drunk in town and the Pony would bring them home.

See that scar on my little finger, I got that at the Shoulder of Mutton about 1909, when I was 8 years of age. A young cousin of mine, a girl, she was the daughter of an uncle named Yardley, they were hairdressers on Chapel Ash and she was washing her dolls clothes. Like a fool I said I would put them through me grandmother's wringer and I put me little finger through with em."

"That was your fathers father then Frank", the Guard asked.

"Yes, me mothers father worked as coachman for Manders the paint people up at the Mount. The most he ever earned was 22 shillings. All his sons worked at the paint works and they got even less, if they asked for a rise in wages old Mander would threaten to sack their old man. He worked there from 13 years of age until he was 68 and he never had a penny as pension. He got a job at the Ministry of Agriculture and Fisheries after he retired and eventually, after the war he got £2-10".

"Times was hard then Frank", the Guard sympathised.

"Arr, if we had an orange and apple and a few nuts for Christmas presents we had done well. I was 15 before I had a broken down old bike, but still we had happy times. I remember one that wasn't very happy though. I had spent weeks looking for a good fork to make a catapult with, then I had to get the money for the elastic etc and eventually I had it finished. It was a real beauty, I was really proud of it. I hadn't finished it more than a couple of days when I was walking up Old Hill just aiming it, you know, not shooting it, and as I passed the police station the sergeant came out, "That's a good catapult Frank", he said, "let have a look at it". I gave it him of course and he said, "Yes it is a good one, I think I best look after that for you, before you get into any trouble with it", and that's the last I ever saw of it, after all that trouble and work".

"Did ya ever ask for it back Frank", I asked.

"Not bloody likely, we knew better than question the police them days matey".

"I left school in 1915, just after the war began, but I didn't start on the railroad then, I got a job at The Sunbeam, they were making aeroplane engines, for the war. The hours were 6am till 6pm for 5 shillings and three pence, that was me wages, me mother had the 5 shillings and I had the three pence. I used to catch the 5-20am tram from Tettenhall to get in for 6am. We had breakfast at 8 till 8-30, dinner 1-

0 till 2-0 and I used to get home just after 7pm. On Fridays we were paid, but not until after we finished at 6pm. There were about 2,000 workers at the Morefield works them days and it took an hour to pay em. When you first started, like me, you had to go to the back of the queue, if you tried to get in early to get ya money first you would get several kicks up the back side until you were at the back of the queue.

I didn't get home until after 8pm on Fridays".

"Were they horse drawn trams then Frank", I asked.

"No! they had them boxes all down the middle of the road and the tram picked up electricity from them, they called it the Lorraine System.

I used to work before that, I had a paper round for years at Bonds, the news paper shop. We used to meet at 6-30am, I delivered 50 daily papers and 150 evening papers all for 6 pence a week. I used to do Upper st, Old Hill, Newbridge, Lower st, Aldersely rd, Sandy Lane, Malthouse Lane, Stockwell End and Danescourt rd all for a tanner.

I didn't stay long at the Sunbeam, I got a job on the railway, on the Dining cars at Birmingham Snow Hill. I was page boy on the Cornishman for three trips and in the hotel at Snow hill at other times. We used to lodge at Penzance on the Cornishman, I had 6 shillings for 3 trips. I remember that when I was in the Hotel at Snow Hill, we used to take trays of sandwiches, door stops we called em, and mugs of tea to the troop trains. We had several train load of Yanks come through one week and they all had a sandwich and a mug of tea, that's a lot of sandwiches and tea ya know.

Anyhow, I got fed up with that so I applied for a transfer to Tyseley Loco Depot as a fireman. I got it almost straight away. I had the most miserable few weeks of my life after that, I was on a saddle tanky with an old Driver about 64, he had a long beard, I knew nothing about the job and he hadn't got a scrap of patience. I wasn't there long because I applied for a move to Stafford Rd.

I hadn't been at Stafford Rd more than a week or two when I was getting a tanky ready in the small shed. I was getting cocky by now thinking that I knew the ropes. While I had been at the stores they had turned the engine out and it was moving slowly along the going out road. I jumped over the pit behind the engine and went to climb aboard while it was moving. There was a lot of steam around the front of the engine and although I could see a steel column, you know the ones, they're still there now. As you know these columns are very close to the engine but I reckoned I could climb aboard before we got to it. Well, I reckoned wrong didn't I. It caught me half way up the steps and there aint no give in them steel pillars I can tell ya.

There was a blinding red flash before me eyes and a pain the like of which I had never known before and don't want to again.

I somehow passed the pillar but my legs were useless and I didn't know where I hurt most.

I fell onto the blue bricks and lay there in awful pain. There were soon plenty of blokes around but every time they tried to move me I had another of those blinding red flashes. I tell you, when you're hurt like that and lying there in pain you are in the loneliest place on earth, no matter how many folk there are around.

Eventually they got me on to that stretcher on wheels which they like to call an ambulance and several mates pushed me all the way to the Royal Hospital. The main roads were paved with those Rowley Cobbles those days and I can tell you that I counted every one we passed over between Stafford rd and the Hospital. It appears that I had broken my pelvis as well as squeezing just about everything in my insides.

It was a long time before I could lie in comfort and longer still before I could walk again. Eventually I was well enough to start work and I called into the Office to tell them. The office blokes were glad to see me back of course but when Old Styles, the Foreman came in, one of the office chaps said,

"This is Frank Jeavons, Mr Styles, the fireman who was crushed against the pillar in the little shed".

"Oh is it", he said, just managing a preoccupied glance, you know, "Well we do need those pillars to keep the roof up you know my boy", and with that he went out.

I realised then that that was all they cared about individuals".

The Guard and I had listened to this tale without interruption. I reflected that not only were the pillars still there and firemen still climbing on to moving engines but there were several other deadly traps in the dust and steam laden shed. On the very road which Frank had just described there was a wall which, if you put your head out at the wrong moment would take it off. The shed and yard were poorly lit, smoke and steam obscured the pits and other traps which lay as thick a daisies in a field.

It's interesting to note that more than 40 years after his injury when Frank retired the pillars still stood awaiting the unwary as did many such hazards many of which could have been remedied quite cheaply. They had been passed over in the hurly burly of the day to day running of the shed. They mostly existed when the contractors came in to start the demolition, a simple fact which gives the lie to the popular belief that the Unions were looking for trouble under every stone, if they had been at Stafford Rd, they wouldn't have known where to start.

Before Frank could continue with his life story, off came the signal and the Guard scrambled down and ran back to his van as we pulled quietly out of the loop.

PARAFFIN LAMPS

"Are well, I can tell yer, that it's been proved time and again that the paraffin lamp is the most reliable lamp it's possible to obtain, tests have proved that".

Most of us nodded apathetically, hiding our astonishment at such a patently obvious load of bull shit being stated as a fact. Non of us were going to contradict big and nasty though. How ever, fireman 'Knowall' had no such inhibitions.

"The bloody paraffin lamps are Whaaat!", he shouted, stringing the final word out in calculated contempt, "A bit of wind and half the headlights between here and Penzanze are out, a battery or dynamo operated light would never go out, they are too expensive to fix, that's the trouble, nuthin else".

"Arr, but that's because the paraffin lamps aint looked after properly", Big and nasty replied with gusto, "It's firemen banging them on the floor to put them out instead of opening the back to blow them out, that what's the cause of that. If they were cleaned and the wicks trimmed like we used to do when we was firemen there would be no trouble at all with paraffin lamps".

Fireman knowall wasn't having that, "Oh we've heard all about you lot, years ago, always taking care of your lamps, wiping down the footplate, carrying the drivers about, some of you lot should get jobs with the angels eventually, you're too good to be true you lot are. The fact remains that the lamps are not going to be looked after are they, everybody ill treats them, I saw you bounce one on the floor yesterday so don't come the high and mighty with us".

Big and nasty was taken aback somewhat, several of us had also seen him bounce the lamps on the floor to put them out only the previous morning but we wasn't going to say so. He was also well known for being a slovenly twat and if he was as clean and efficient when he was a young fireman, as he liked to make out, then he had certainly changed a lot, but the truth was, as fireman 'Knowall' had pointed out, that the lamps were not going to be nurse maided so the damn things were a pain in the whatsit.

Big and Nasty was not the man to take the truth lying down so after a short think he came back with, "You can say what you like, but tests have proved that paraffin lamps are the most reliable lamps for railway use that money can buy".

Fireman knowall was openly contemptuous of this statement, "When?" he demanded, "When did these tests take place and what sort of lamps did they test them against.

I have heard talk of these tests for years but no bugger seems to know when they took place or any details about them what-so-ever. Come on, I'll bet you a fiver that you can't tell me when these tests took place or what types of lamps were tested alongside them. And don't give me a load of bull shit because I shall make enquiries about any date you give".

Big and nasty was outraged, at this stage he would normally have started to issue physical threats to get his own way but fireman 'Knowall' was tall and pretty well built and also not averse to a touch of violence. Bearing this in mind, Big and nasty decided against threats.

"I don't know what date these tests were, but there are plenty of our chaps that do, ask some of em", he spluttered, obviously beat for something to say.

'Knowall' was not going to let him off that lightly, "Look here, my old man has had a car nearly twenty years and the lights are still working now, and, he doesn't have to keep buying paraffin. He has never had a new dynamo, only two batteries and a couple of bulbs in all that time, there's no comparison, that's what I say".

Big and Nasty was trying hard to think of some way of turning the argument in his favour when 'Short and softly spoken' walked in, he caught the last few words of 'Knowalls' conversation, "What was that", he asked.

"We were just talking about the lamps on these engines" 'Knowall' informed him.

"I'll tell yer one thing", said softly spoken, softly, "There's no finer and more reliable lamp in the world for railway work than the paraffin lamp, tests have proved it time and again".

'Knowall' stared for a second in total disbelief then with a string of naughty words he left the cabin.

My Father James (Jimmy) Brown as a young fireman at Ludlow Station 1923.

Although I worked at Stafford Road and Oxley Shed for 12 years, 10 as a fireman I, sadly, have no Photo's of myself. It was not 'the thing to do' those days, in fact I find that most of the Photographs of the engines and men which do exist are mainly of the 1950s. It was then that men belatedly realised that it was all sliding away and soon there would be nothing to photograph.

By that time I was in another place with my mind on other things.

The famous engine 999 Sir Alexander standing in the lower yard Stafford Road in readiness for the Royal Train. This 7 foot single wheeler achieved a mileage of 1,329,000 on the W'ton to London expresses between 1880 and 1904 when it was withdrawn.

Side Tanky in Kidderminster Station about the turn of the century. The driver standing on the framing is the Father of Ted Body to whom I owe the privilege of using Photos Nos 1,2, 5, & 6. Ted's father came from Truro Cornwall to the midlands before the turn of the century. Ted was himself a Fireman and Driver at Wolverhampton throughout his career.

Shunters at Oxley Sidings, displaying the alert fitness without which their job is impossible.

Sunday morning on the Cannock Road Shunter. Clean overalls but shattered.

Ernie Rossiter and Ted Body Share a drink at the 45th anniversary of the introduction of the 'Kings' at Tysely. The King, 6000 was shipped to the USA in the 20s and the well known Bell was fitted there to commemorate the event.

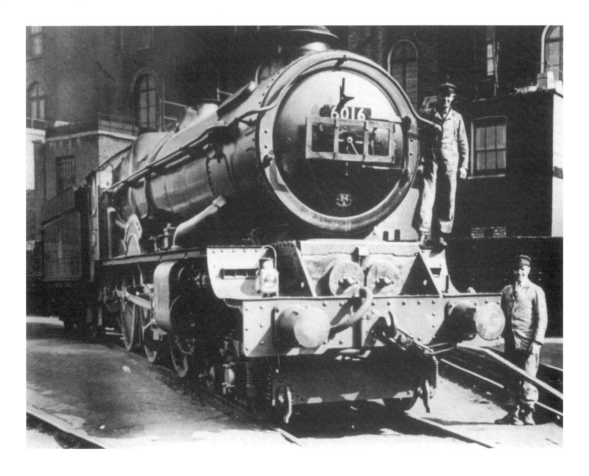

Ted Body and Chris Powell At Ranelagh Bridge, where all express engines into Paddington were turned, tanks filled, coal pulled down while the crew had a short break before the return journey. Notice the closeness of the flats, the smoke and noise was often the cause of trouble with the residents.

From left to right; Dave Newall, Fred Lott, Simon Latham, Geoff Brown, Phil Jones, Friends of the Trevithic on foot-plate of the "Rocket" on the day when it was my priviledge and pleasure to fire and even drive it.
Photo by Mike Mathews

The author working the replica 1802 Trevithick engine, designed by Richard Trevithick and built at Coalbrookdale. This engine is owned by The Ironbridge Gorge Museums. Run by Phillip Jones and the Friends of the Trevithick it can be seen working one week end each month throughout the summer. The occasion pictured is the visit of the replica Stephenson Rocket from York Railway Museum. Photo by Trevor Howard.

RICHARD TREVITHICK

Richard Trevithick was almost certainly Britains most important inventor of the 19th century. It was, without much doubt, his natural inventiveness and determination which put British Engineering at least 30years ahead of all other countries.

As a child he had little formal education but prefered to learn by watching the miners and the engineers who abounded in his native Cornwall. From the start everyone he came into contact were impressed by his ability and ideas. The inspiration which would later build the worlds first steam locomotives and envisage a host of other inventions was already there long before he had the actual opportunity to build them.

His great misfortune was that he was inspired with countless inventions many years before the technology existed to display them to their full potential.

Within many of us lies the power to alter and improve that which already exists, that which has been invented and proved by someone else, but the true magic is in the heart and mind of the human who sees an idea in his own imagination and even though others scoff possess's the courage, the determination and self belief to overcome all critism and every obstacle. To work selflessly towards an end that is of value to his fellow man and to find in that work it's own reward so that if that work is undervalued and the credit stolen from him that man can go on undaunted because the love of life and work are reward enough.

Such a man was RICHARD TREVITHICK. The greatest and yet the most undervalued of all the great 19th century engineers.

ERNIE

It was about 5 am on a cold, spring morning in 1944. Stafford Rd Locomotive Shed was a hive of activity, every set of rails held a steam engine being prepared for duty. My mate and I had been hard at it for some hours.The shed foreman had asked us to prepare a Castle for a special train. The Castle was outside and this made preparation difficult. We found the huge steam engine with hardly any steam, and with smoke and flame belching from its' firehole doors. But now, after a long and sweaty slog she stood in full steam, a good fire, coal all cracked into useable lumps and the foot-plate clean and shining. The boards were all washed down and steaming in the firelight as we handed over to Charlie and his mate.

As we shouted "So long!" and they pulled slowly off the shed, we decided that a cup of tea was in order so we made our way over to the canteen. Walking up to the counter to collect our cuppa, we noticed that 'Ern' was holding forth.

Ern was an engine driver at Stafford Rd Shed. A number of his fellow locomen were sitting around him in various states of disinterest. Some looked vaguely alert as if they expected to be amused, others had that pained and disenchanted attitude of men who'd heard it all before. We sat near enough to hear, but far enough away to avoid any involvement because Ern was well known for starting an argument, and when he did, he didn't mind who he dragged into it.

You couldn't miss Ern, where ever he was he was easy to spot. Even in the far distance, you couldn't doubt his identity. His long, gesticulating arms, his lean and slightly stooped figure were a dead giveaway. Even more distinctive though, were his quick, determined movements, his accusing finger and wild, abandoned manner as he argued hotly (which he always did) about every subject under the sun.

He would wave his arms about while looking in all directions. His cloth cap, unable to cope with the speed of his head would turn by degrees until the peak was immediately above his right ear. This sideways looking cap over his staring eyes and lean and angry face gave him a manic, almost lunatic appearance which could be most intimidating.

Ern was a World War One veteran, and he was never so wild as when recounting his wartime experiences when, as he never tired of telling us, he and his mates were always either starving, wet through, freezing cold or frightened to death; and often all of these at one time.

Sometimes, when men have been through such harrowing experiences it leaves them a little withdrawn and reluctant to get involved in avoidable disputes. Not so our Ern, he had an extremely short fuse and would enter into any and every dispute at the drop of a hat. Neither did he have time for red-tape or petty officialdom. The outcome was that Ern was often to be found at the very centre of a rumpus. He also had what was, for a footplateman, a cardinal sin: a record of poor punctuality which was second to none. Despite these and many other drawbacks, Ern was quite well liked.

This was probably because he was outspoken, forthright and often most amusing, qualities which most men admired. To illustrate this point, there was at Stafford Rd, a loco shed foreman who was noted for his ignorant and unsympathetic attitude towards staff who were late on duty; especially young firemen, and at that time Ern was a young fireman.

This foreman had repeatedly warned Ern about his late comings and he nearly exploded when Ern told him by way of an excuse, that owing to an early morning mist he couldn't see the time by the church clock. At that time Ern lived in sight of the church clock, you see.

"What the hell's the matter with your own soddin' clock?" this foreman demanded.

"Ain't got a bugger," Ern replied. "Just married, can't afford one yet."

The foreman was speechless, but it says a lot about the impression Ern made, that just as everyone was convinced that he was about to be sacked, the foreman presented him with an alarm clock saying, "And for Christ's sake, try to get here on time in future."

Despite his generally amusing disposition Ern was cursed with that unfortunate trait, not uncommon amongst his generation, of being totally blind to anyone else's point of view. He was quite capable of giving a piercing analysis of all British Rail's problems and their solutions, but he seemed to think that all the onerous regulations and penalties clearly needed to carry them through would only apply to others. This point had been well illustrated only a few weeks before.

Several sets of us (a set being a driver, fireman and guard) were sitting in the Zone cabin awaiting the supervisor's pleasure. I should explain that trains were so disorganised during this time that many of the normal schedules were abandoned completely and so a number of sets of men were booked on without any specific job. These men were the charges of the Zone Supervisor, who would deploy them as and when they were needed. This offered a pleasing variety of work, but had the serious drawback of being totally unpredictable with regards to hours worked.

It was common for men to sit playing cards or telling the tale for hours on end, then when the better part of the shift was over to be sent on some job which would mean long hours. Twelve to sixteen hours was quite normal. If you were looking for a fat wage packet, this was fine, but if you had plans for your spare time it could be infuriating.

The resultant confusion and disagreements are easy to imagine. Anyway, one of the occupants of the cabin was Ern. He had been through several issues of national importance already, and I think I could say that we were all well aware of his standpoint on all of these. He'd then stretched out on a bench to enjoy two hours of sleep, for which we were nearly as grateful as he was. On waking he cadged himself a cup of tea whilst easing himself quietly back into the land of the living. He then settled down to sit out the next hour or so after which he could confidently expect the supervisor to send him home on seven hours. It was all very satisfactory as far as Ern was concerned, anyone could see that.

At this point, some joker began to tell of a young fireman who had defied all authority to come home passenger from Crewe rather than work a goods train which would have certainly meant him working considerable overtime. Some of those assembled thought this young man was quite justified, and praised his courage in facing up to the issue. Others were opposed to such rebellious action, Ern was now fully refreshed and ready for action.

"What sort of a railroad do ya think it is then, when a young bit of a kid can defy experienced men, old enough to be his father!" he shouted. "How are ya goin to keep things moving if every bugger does as he likes?" Then, before anyone could get a word in, he went on. "We'll get nowhere with this railroad until we get some discipline back into the job, I can tell yer. Until we get back to how it was before the war, when we all had to do as we were told we shall do no good" he spluttered. "When they said jump, in those days we bloody well jumped, and don't you forget it."

One or two of Ern's mates who'd known him before the war were making no effort to hide their amazement at the pot calling the kettle black but Ern hardly noticed. His cap was slewed around, his eyes were blazing and he was going great guns. In case we hadn't heard him the first time, he shouted again. "You've got to have soddin' discipline to run a railroad and until the foreman can give orders and know they'll be obeyed, we'll do no good" he hooted, banging the table with his fist. "NO ARGUMENTS! NO MESSIN', ON YER BIKE!"

That very second the cabin door burst open. It was the Zone Supervisor, Westbury Fred. "Ern, could you pop down the branch junction to relieve a train of tanks?"

"Not at this bloody time of day I won't" Ern exploded. "I'll see you in hell first!"

The whole cabin erupted and fell about laughing at this sudden about face.

Ern was completely baffled by their response. After all, the need for discipline among the rabble was self evident to all except this bunch of idiots, but as to his present position, well, there had to be sense and reason in all things, and after all, 'he was Ern'.

From all this you can gather that he was a strange and unpredictable character and I don't think I could do him justice in another ten pages, so I'll continue.

Now where were we? Oh yes, we were in the canteen and Ern was telling us about the time that he and his mate had just been to Aberystwith on a Cambrian Coast Excursion. Some of the track to 'Aber' was single line. Changing staffs and stopping at all the holiday stations made it quite a long trip, so the train crew would often be booked for a short break then work back later.

Because the weather was nice, Ern and his mate had supped a jar or two and strolled around 'Aber' for some hours and were now approaching Welshpool on the return journey. The day had been long and hot, and Ern was clapped out. The years in the trenches had left him with feet which would have been an asset to no man. At this stage of the trip his feet were slipping about in a welter of sweat and his toes were throbbing something awful.

It was Ern's regular practice while filling the tank at Welshpool, to dangle his bare feet in the icy water. You might find this a trifle surprising. I certainly did, but Ern swore by it. Anyway, with this moment of ecstasy in mind and because his feet were in a particularly bad way, he began to remove his shoes and socks. He did this sitting on his hard wooden seat with the engine throwing him first one way then the other. He then stuffed the sweat soaked socks in the shoes before placing them on the tool box to catch the cool air stream sweeping across the tender.

The engine was passing over the river bridge on the approach to the station. The engine was certainly not a smooth runner, and the driver may have been coming in a little faster than usual, but whatever the reason, the tender gave a sudden lurch and Ern's socks and shoes went over the side to go tumbling down into the river. ERN - WAS - WICKED !

He let go a howl that you could hear for miles. "Me shoes, me bloody shoes", he hooted, poking the busy driver frantically on the shoulder. The driver looked around with a look of pre-occupied surprise on his face. "What's the matter with ya floppin shoes?" he asked.

"They're floating down the soddin' river, ain't they, and no wonder. It's a marvel we ain't in there with 'em, the way you were coming in!"

The driver was not unnaturally bewildered by all this but in between applications of the brake, he did manage to say how sorry he was, but he hadn't been used to his mates removing their socks and shoes whilst firing an express train. His voice had a nasty, sarcastic edge to it which riled Ern no end.

As always when things went wrong, Ern was trying to blame anyone other than himself. He was using naughty words and demanding that the driver find an immediate solution to his predicament. The driver, on the other hand, (being only too well acquainted with Ern's little ways) felt no such urgency.

As Ern recounted all this to a canteen full of bantering mates, one wag was heard to remark dryly, "I should keep quiet about that if I was you, Ern. What I can remember of your socks you could be prosecuted for poisoning the river."

Ern soon told him that if he had had a dose of the trenches, he wouldn't be so quick to open his face. But back in Welshpool, Ern was filling the tank in his bare feet. His temper was vile and he was still blaming the driver for the whole affair. His mate was not impressed but being a practical man, he did suggest (in between non-committal grunts)

"See if the Bobby's got a spare pair of old boots to get ya home and I'll finish filling the tank!"

I must explain here that a signalman's job is very hard indeed on footwear. In order to pull the signals and points over, it's necessary to place one foot on the curve of the frame and pull really hard. This, over a long period, does the most astonishing things to a perfectly good pair of boots or shoes. The constant pressure in one direction pushes the upper from the sole until the footwear is barely recognisable.

Because of this, 'Bobby's' always kept a pair of old shoes in the signal box especially to wear at work. Eventually these were discarded in favour of a newer pair. This resulted in a locker containing an assortment of incredibly misshapen footwear which could be found in most signal boxes. It was into just such a locker that Ern was invited to search. By this time the Guard was about to wave his green flag so Ern grabbed a couple of pairs and scampered back to the engine. Well, you do scamper a bit in bare feet.

So off they went with barefoot Ern firing the engine and living in mortal dread of a lump of coal rolling onto his swollen toes. In between shovelling coal, working the injectors, watching for signals and exchanging staffs, he was trying to get those shoes on. According to Ern, (and I believe him) those shoes were in a terrible state. In the years that they had occupied the used shoe locker, the leather had gone as hard as a walnut shell. It's doubtful whether the original owner could have worn those shoes, even after soaking them in vinegar overnight. So for Ern, who had awkward feet anyway and didn't even know what size they were, it was hopeless. Mind you, he didn't give up easily, not Ern. He sprayed them with scalding water from the pet pipe, then laid into them with the coal pick and battered them this way and that with the shovel.

All this only served to distort the shoes further until, in a fit of temper he threw them overboard coming down Shifnal Bank. After an eternity of discomfort, Ern and his mate were rolling down the slope towards Cannock Rd bridge. His mate suggested that as Ern's route home lay along the Cannock Rd, he might like to drop off by the bridge. This was quite a kindly gesture, because the Driver would have to take the tools in and book Ern off, not the sort of things that this particular Driver normally did and it would avoid Ern being seen and mercilessly lampooned by countless locomen.

There was no sign of gratitude from Ern as his sore feet trod gingerly down the steel steps. He still blamed the Driver for the whole affair. Nevertheless, here he was in the dark, the sounds of his engine dying away and about two miles separating him from his bed. Most people were in their beds, and Ern was grateful for that, but with a long and painful walk home still to come, Ern was not a happy man.

Anyone with a persevering and inventive nature would almost certainly have devised some method of wrapping their feet to avoid further pain and damage, but whatever was the exact opposite of perseverance and inventiveness, Ern was it. By the time he had scrambled up the pebble and nettle strewn bank onto the Cannock Rd he was feeling the most exquisite pain at every step.

Now you may think that the pavement along the Cannock Rd was quite an easy walk, and with shoes and socks on so it was, but to Ern every step was full of dread. His eyes searched out every square inch of pavement as they never had before. By now his feet were in a dreadful state and the mere thought of stepping on a sharp stone or stubbing his toe on a slab produced waves of terror.

Never had he walked with such stealth. Nevertheless, anyone lying awake that night with the window open would have heard Ern. Oh yes, many a naughty word was spoken along the silent streets that night. By the time he was approaching Park Lane, he was stopping every few steps for a cough and a drag and a cuss. There was only one thing that Ern was grateful for and that was the absence of folk to witness his ridiculous predicament.

However, even this modest blessing was soon denied him, for who should come riding by on his shining bicycle but one of His Majesty's constables. From their attitudes, you would not have guessed it but this constable and Ern were well known to each other. The constable had seen fit to have words with Ern on a number of occasions. Minor things such as riding a bike without lights, that sort of thing. There were times when only the constable's forbearance had saved Ern from prosecution because his manner was always surly and aggressive.

In fact it would be fair comment to say that Ern hated this copper. He tried to walk as casually as he possibly could while the copper rode by, and he breathed a sigh of relief when he reckoned that the danger was past because he was in no mood to bandy words with this 'stupid flat-foot'. However, his relief was short-lived because he suddenly became aware of a 'presence' nearby. Out of the corner of his eye, he could just make out the front tyre of the copper's bike. He could also hear the faint whirring of a well-oiled free wheel.

To Ern, whose bike was always rusty, neglected and breaking down, things like well-oiled free wheels were a source of intense irritation, and what with the state of his feet and everything, he was very testy indeed. He tried to walk with a touch of nonchalance, but all he could manage was a grotesque and painful hobble. The constable was in no hurry to open the conversation. He was looking on with the mild and natural curiosity of a man who has just spotted another adult male walking the streets at 2 am in his bare feet.

A number of times Ern stopped to ease his agony, always looking towards the terraced housing on his left. Not once did he show signs of the copper's presence, but the copper knew better and he was quite comfy, gliding forward on his silent rubber tyres, then stopping with one foot resting gently on the pavement each time Ern rested.

Eventually, Ern could stand it no longer.

"What's the matter with you, copper?" he snarled, "Haven't you ever seen a bloke's feet before?" The Constable leaned on his handle-bars whilst considering this statement most carefully.

"Can't say I've ever seen a bloke out in the small hours in his bare feet, Ern, is it a new fashion coming about then?" This was said in a calm but distinct voice normally used for the feeble-minded.

"What", Ern exploded, "What! Is it a bloody crime then to walk the streets without shoes on? Haven't you got any burglars to catch, or any kids without lights on their bikes that you can chase? Are you lockin' people up for not havin' shoes on their feet?"

The copper was enjoying this immensely. "Just for the record Ern," he inquired, "why ARE you walking the streets barefoot in the early hours. I have to ask. After all, there could be a boot or shoe thief about."

He then had to caution Ern, in no uncertain terms, about his language, but even in the midst of Ern's tirade he could see the situation was pretty desperate. Suddenly and firmly he said, "Shut up Ern", Ern went silent, more in surprise than obedience.

"Get on the crossbar" the copper said.

Ern could not believe his ears. It WAS the early hours of the morning, and though he had less than half a mile to go, he was in desperate straits. Even so, the idea of this mortal enemy of his, an officer of the law, no less, giving him a lift on the crossbar of his bike was surely a joke?

The Constable was losing patience. "Do you want a bloody lift home or not?" he snarled.

Once having glimpsed a solution to his problem, Ern was hooked. He had suddenly savoured the thought of his poor tortured feet off the ground while the Constable pedalled him swiftly and painlessly home. He wasn't going to let such a chance escape, so without another word he laid his tired bottom on the crossbar and the Constable's uniformed arms closed around him and mercy of mercies, they began to glide softly and oh so peacefully and painlessly towards Ern's abode.

He gripped the handlebars tightly, the Constable's grunting breaths brushed his ear as they wobbled their way around the corner of Park Lane and climbed the first gentle rise, but soon the Constable's strong legs urged the heavily loaded bike along and in no time at all they stopped outside Ern's house.

Ern dismounted in silence and although he couldn't think of a time when anyone had performed such a much needed service for him, and he was truly grateful, he still couldn't quite bring himself to say 'thank you' to this copper. At the gate of his house he stopped, looked around and nodded grimly towards the copper in what was a semblance of 'thanks'.

The copper did the same but not a word was spoken.

The Constable turned his bike in the direction they'd just come and pedalled off without a word.

Ern hobbled painfully up the garden path and as he pushed his key into the lock with immense relief, you might have seen, had you looked really closely, the suggestion of a smile on Ern's face.

A sight as rare as a swallow in winter.

THE ELASTICITY OF HIGH PRESSURE STEAM

Steam is an immensely powerful and elastic gas, yes a gas.

When I say steam, I don't refer to that wet and wafting vapour which we see circling most steam engines or coming from our kettles. This is not steam but water vapour, the very fact that you can see it denies that it is steam. Steam is that dry, invisible, powerful and elastic gas which can only survive for moments unless confined in an immensely strong pressure vessel, which is usually also a boiler. It is immensely powerful and dangerous. Allow it to build up into high pressure in a vessel too weak to hold it, and a massive explosion can and has occurred. Once in contact with human skin and it will peel it off in seconds. Only modern regulations formed by years of bitter experience keep it safe.

The higher the temperature and pressure, the more powerful and elastic it is. On modern steam engines the steam is passed from the boiler along heating tubes known as 'Superheaters' to raise the temperature still higher and create an even 'Drier' and more elastic gas.

This highly elastic gas which we call steam is then ready for use. It passes from the 'super heaters' to the steam chest. The flow of steam from the steam chest to cylinder is controlled by the valve. This is usually a double piston which controls the timing and volume of steam to the cylinder.

When the engine is moving the valve first allows a small amount of steam to enter the front end of the cylinder just before the piston reaches the end of it's stroke. This is known as lead steam and it cushions the piston and assists it on its return, giving a smooth action. The timing of this is critical.

Next the valve begins to open fully pushing the piston on its journey by the direct force of boiler pressure. Then the valve closes again to allow the steam to continue its work by sheer expansion. Finally the valve opens to exhaust and allows the steam to flash through the open valve and up the blast pipe and chimney.

The valve then opens to lead steam at the opposite end of the cylinder and the whole thing starts again.

Now come with us on a just a short section of the trip from Wolverhampton to Paddington. Imagine we have just picked up water at Kings Sutton and now we are streaking around Aynho Junction at 70 miles per hour. The fireman begins to shovel as the King class engine lays into 15 eight wheelers up the bank to Ardley.

Once up the bank the sides of the cutting gradually fall away as our speed increases. As the speed increases so the driver reduces the travel of the valve and with it the amount of steam reaching the cylinder.

In less than a minute we are passing the distant signal for Bicester and now we can see for miles around. The speed of the engine is now increasing every second, 80 - 85 - 90 - 95 and if all is going well maybe the magic ton, 100 miles per hour.

On the platform at Bicester a small crowd of passengers await the stopper which follows our train. With us travelling at about 100mph, what will they see?

They will stare in open mouthed wonder as the massive locomotive hurtles towards them, the bogies dancing and the exhaust roaring. The pistons and rods are just a silver blurr.
But what of that piston now?

How fast is that streaking piston moving at that moment?

How long, does it take for the flashing piston to complete one stroke?
I can't ask you to imagine that time span, it's impossible for the human brain to picture such a micro span of time, but we can appreciate it, marvel at it.

If we take one brief second from our lives and and divide it, then divide it again, and again, in fact divide it sixteen times. Our piston stroke is faster by far than the time we have left. That piston is quicker by far than the glint on the surface of a pool, or the crack of a dry twig.

But no matter how fast the piston moves the steam is faster still, in that micro dot of time, that steam is in there to cushion the blow, it is there to force the flashing piston on, there to expand with savage insistence, and there to exhaust like a rocket and lead again.

THAT, - IS THE MAGIC, - THE EXPLOSIVE POWER AND ELASTICITY OF -
HIGH PRESSURE, - SUPER HEATED,- STEAM.

DIPLOMAT

We were waiting for the train to Wednesbury, for some reason which has been lost in the mists of time, I was with a mate I shall call Diplomat. I call him that with just a hint of sarcasm because that's exactly what he was not. He was not a bad mate really, in fact at times, he could be very supportive. He was a shortish thick set chap who somehow always looked older than his years. This was probably because he took life so seriously, particularly railway work or politics, but most things really. He seemed incapable of accepting anyone else's point of view as a matter of course. Instead he would use every argument it was possible to imagine to convert all and sundry to his rather narrow outlook.

As most men were highly resistant to changing their minds, especially when being harassed, he was spectacularly unsuccessful. This was not an unusual situation among Loco men, but he also had a very short fuse and would begin to slate even the most genial of men if their argument didn't match his own.

He would say things like, "I don't think you know what you are talking about mister!", or, "If I was you mister I should keep my mouth shut and save making a fool of me'self". These were not humorous little asides but pieces of serious advice delivered in a rather overbearing manner. Never the less, as my politics roughly matched his own, 'Diplomat' amd I rubbed along quite nicely.

I was not his regular mate but for some reason, again, lost in the mists of time, I was taking the place of his mate on one of the Wednesbury shunters. I had purchased two daily papers with wildly different political views and the moment we settled into the compartment of this non corridor coach I began to read and was soon lost in the politics of the day. It was holiday time and the train was unusually full with families going out for the day. When we left Low Level, there weren't many empty compartments, but by the time we had picked up still more holiday makers at Preistfield, ours was about the only compartment with vacant seats.

I was too deep in the newspaper to notice much as we ran into Bilston but I was vaguely aware that several parties were having difficulties in finding seats. One of these parties consisted of two extremely large raw boned blokes who, I found out later, were from the steel mills at Bilston. They were with their wives or young ladies and were clearly out for a good time on this clear sunny summers day. Eventually they decided that the only compartment left was ours and opened the door and climbed in. Now while they had been searching up and down the platform for seats they had seen us occupying a compartment to ourselves and made some comment like, "No wonder we can't get on the soddin train, it's full of railway men". Now I believe that they said something like that, but I was never entirely sure, because I was so engrossed in my newspaper that I heard nothing, but 'Diplomat' did, and it was more than his flesh and blood could stand to let such an harmless comment pass.

The two young couples settled them selves down and began to chat in the excited, pleasant and inconsequential way that people do when they are out for the day. They looked as astonished as I was myself when 'Diplomat' suddenly began to tell them, in no uncertain terms, what he thought of "People who make snide remarks about two men who were keeping the nations vital services going while half the country was off enjoying themselves."

The burly steel worker nearest to me was not a man to be spoken to like that so he began by pointing out that, "It was people like him who paid our wages and in fact, if it wasn't for people like him and his companions, the likes of us would be on the dole and a good job too".

'Diplomat' retorted with an unnecessarily long and overbearing case for our journey being far more important than theirs, in fact he made it appear that if we didn't get to Wednesbury, to man the shunter, then the nation might collapse, and these burly steel workers and their mates would have no work to go back to after enjoying themselves.

Burly steel worker began to say some rather nasty things about railway men who travelled in the same compartments as people in their best clothes, and that instead we should travel in the guards van or have a couple of wagons put on the back for us. In the following argument he did include one or two quite naughty words which shocked his lady companions more than they did us, but never the less 'Diplomat' took the most unnecessary exception to them.

Well, I will not continue with the dialogue which hurtled back and forth across that compartment but suffice to say that despite the short distance between Bilston and Wednesbury these two men had managed to work this discussion into a furious slanging match which was completely out of control and was causing the two women folk to have a fit of the vapours. It had not escaped my notice that the good lady who accompanied the massive hunk next to me was really worried and saying things like, "Now now George, calm down, he's an old man, don't start now". This should have been a warning to my mate that this man probably had a history of violence, but he seemed oblivious to all such silly caution.

I looked out of the train window at this point and realised that if 'Diplomat' had reckoned on arriving at Wednesbury before this bloke boiled over he was going to be disappointed. We were going over the bridge which marked the start of the falling incline into Wednesbury, but given the growing row that was threatening to explode any minute, it seemed a million miles away. Suddenly, just as 'Diplomat' was about to open his mouth to heap coals on the fire Burly George blew his top. He rose to his feet and leaned over my mate who's face, by comparison with that of the hulk who towered over him, looked about the size of a shirt button, and began to issue threats.

To give my mate his due, he appeared to remain calm, or frozen or sommat as George shouted in a voice which deafened me and the rest of the coach I should think. "Shut it!" he bawled, "Shut it, this minute or I'll put this in ya face".

The two women tried to calm him but they were like a couple of butterflies fluttering in the middle of a battle field, they had no chance.

'Diplomat' went to move his lips again, I know because I was sitting right opposite and I saw, with horror, his lips twich, but before he could utter a sound Burly George bellowed, "Shut it! I've told yer, shut it! or I'll fill your face for good".

As he said this he held a massive horney fist at the ready while pointing at 'Diplomat's' face with the finger of his other hand. No one had ever known 'Diplomat' to stay silent in such circumstances in all his life and he hardly seemed likely to start now. I don't mind saying that I was really frightened by now. After all, he was my mate, and he was a lot older than this massive brute who was threatening him.

In my opinion 'Diplomat' deserved to be put in his place for once, but if Big George carried out his threat he was going to have his features re-arranged as well.

The terrifying question was, what was I going to do about it, I was nearer George's age, but that was about the only advantage I had. In every other respect I felt about as inadequate as a sparrow attacking a Golden Eagle. Never the less, if he attacked my mate I should have to do something, but what. I had an unrivalled view of big George's fist and his finger pointing at 'Diplomat's' nose. The finger looked to me like a small gnarled tree trunk, and the fist hardly bore looking at. For me to punch that huge head from the sitting position and in my fragile state, would have been like a Blue Bottle bunting a Buffalo.

Three times I saw 'Diplomat's' lip tremble and the mouth begin to open, each time burly George raised his fist. His manner, and the look of abject horror on the face of the two women left me in no doubt that he meant to carry out his threat. Never did that bit of railroad between Wednesbury North box and the station seem so distant. Never the less, eventually we felt the brakes go on and we drew to a stand in Wednesbury station. 'Diplomat' and myself opened the door and alighted with tightly buttoned lips under the glowering face and threatening fist of this man, who, I am grateful to say I have never met since.

We walked a few yards along the platform with George's final curses ringing in our ears and the astonished stares of the guard adding to our embarrassment. The guard waved his flag and the train began to move, 'Diplomat' turned and shouted one or two parting insults at Big George who lowered his hand to the door handle and for one awesome second I though he was going to leap from the moving train and chase us. He didn't though and if he had, he certainly wouldn't have caught me, I couldn't answer for my mate though.

When the train was disappearing from view, 'Diplomat' stared at me and said in an accusetorial manner, "You didn't say a lot did you".

"No", I replied with a touch of a sneer, "You said enough for both of us I reckon". To give him his due, he appeared completely unaffected by this nasty incident and apart from that one short accusation he never refered to it again.

BLAENAU FESTINIOG

It was 1947. Snow had lay on the ground for nearly a month and it had frozen every night. Each time that the 'freeze up' appeared to be easing, back it came again with ever more snow and ice. It seemed that each night was worse then the one before. By the time in question, many remote roads and railway branch lines had been blocked for days. Vital coal supplies were cut off, the supplies to towns and power stations were dwindling. Almost every home in Britain relied on coal for heating, and the power stations were almost all coal fired. As supplies of coal dwindled, power was cut off to large areas of Britain. The midlands with it's mass of industry was particularly badly hit with almost one million workers idle.

During the war, people had grown accustomed to managing on meagre rations, but those rations had always been there, now, supplies of everything were threatened. It was in the midst of all this chaos that Sid had a message that the Superintendent wanted to see him. Inspector Barlow shoved his head around the door and said, "Clapham, the Super wants to see you, now!"

"Right Barlow!", Sid replied with just a nice touch of contempt, they were not very chummy. Sid obeyed, his footsteps echoing along the wide passage to the door marked, 'Mr Webb, Superintendent of the Line', he knocked.

"Come in"

"Clapham sir" Sid said smartly.

"Oh, sit down Clapham", replied Mr Webb. This was the normal form of address between men of differing ranks. No Christian names, in fact if Mr Webb had looked up one morning and said to Sid, "Good morning Sid, how are you", Sid's legs would have gone all wobbly. Never the less, there was considerable mutual respect between them.

'Webby' began, (he was always known as 'Webby' behind his back) "You know that most of the branch lines in the division have been blocked for some days, and many important towns and villages are completely cut off".

Sid nodded.

"You also know I'm sure that we have a new snow plough which has been scientifically designed to throw the snow clear of the line so efficiently that it can be used at fairly high speed".

Again Sid merely nodded.

"This plough has been very successful in opening, and keeping open, the main lines. It had been envisaged that it would be used only for the main lines but the situation in North Wales is becoming desperate, and it cannot be allowed to continue. So I want you to go down to Wrexham, there is an engine with the plough attached coming from Chester, you will meet them at Croes Newydd and proceed to Bala where I should like you to find accommodation. I have to ask you to stay there as long as it takes to first, clear the line to Dolgelau, and then the branches, any questions".

Sid thought for a moment or two before saying, "With every respect Sir, most of my experience of railway work has been on the main line under very different conditions to those that apply on those branch lines. I'm sure there are men more competent than me to handle a job like this. There's also the problem of accommodation, things are not easy even for the people living down there, I believe that they have neither food or power at the moment".

"I take your point Clapham", Webby went on immediately, "We have considered these factors but I want a man on the job who has the sense of urgency and the authority to give the opening of these lines top priority. I'm not asking you to tell anyone how to do their job but we must see that the most appropriate men and the most suitable equipment is applied without delay, those lines must be cleared".

"Yes Sir" said Sid.

"As for accommodation, I shall be in touch with the shed foreman and traffic inspector at Bala to ask them for every assistance in finding food and accommodation for you. I'm sure that, given the urgency of the situation they will find something. Thank you Clapham, best wishes for the job, good day to you".

Sid was suddenly out in the passage again with his coat and boots feeling a damn sight heavier than when he went in. He caught the bus home to pack a suitcase and explain to his wife that he was off to North Wales and didn't know when he would be back or where he would be staying. She didn't like it one little bit, well, he never thought she would, but his choice was clear. He could go, or refuse the job which would, to all intents and purposes be the end of his managerial career. He had no intention of making such a far reaching move without much thought, so, he had to go.

On arrival at Wrexham he reported to the foreman, it was mid afternoon by now and growing colder by the minute. The foreman told him that the snow plough was on it's way, "I've told them to put the biggest tender engine which is allowed over the branch lines, I thought it would give you the maximum power and save having to keep stopping for coal and water".

"Sounds sensible to me", Sid admitted

By the time the Chester man had arrived with the plough, and they had picked up a pilot man for the branch line, and backed on to a guards van, it was pitch dark and cold enough for a dozen brass monkeys.

The Wrexham pilot man warned them all to watch out for icicles in the tunnel. It was a timely warning because the tunnel had not been used for days and sharp spikes of ice hung down from the roof of the tunnel, some of them were 4" thick and weighing a hundred weight.

As the van rattled through, the crashing of ice sounded like a thousand windows being smashed. They all stayed safe in the cab of the guards van thanks to the advice of the driver. They were soon at Bala station, the entire town was in completed darkness, it had never been darker, not even at the height of the wartime black out.

There was an air of depression about. After a long hard winter, to be without light, and very little food was not what the population of Bala had been looking forward to. When Sid talked to the Shed Foreman and the Station Master about food and accommodation, they shook their heads, "Oh I don't see you having any chance of that at the moment, we are cut off ourselves, you see, the roads are all blocked", the foreman said, "The powers off, there isn't a morsel of food to spare in the whole of Bala and I should be wasting your time and mine looking Sid, that's my opinion anyway".

Sid was getting very frustrated by now, the situation was only what he had expected and he felt annoyed to think that he had been sent on this job without proper arrangements being made. He wasn't showing any immediate enthusiasm for the job and the Chester driver, who had no right to comment what so ever, misread the signs completely and said, "You know what I think".

No one really cared but they all listened, "I think that you are bloody well frightened of the job", he said directly to Sid

Sid ignored this statement for the moment then said to the foreman, "I'm not about to stop here without food, as for accommodation, I can sleep in the guards van, I know I'll be warm enough there, but if there's no guarantee of a reasonable amount of food each day, then forget it.

I'm going back to Wolverhampton to arrange for a supply of food, and I shall be back here tomorrow". Then he turned to the Chester driver and said, "You mate, can go back to Chester where you came from, and I don't want to see you again, just thank your lucky stars that it's me Sid Clapham you said that to. If it had been some of my colleagues you would have been seeing the Superintendent on Monday. Let me give you a little advice, don't fall foul of me in the future, or you will live to regret it".

Sid then managed to get to Ruabon in time to catch the last passenger and spend the night in his own bed. Next morning he explained the situation at Bala to Webby.

Webby asked, "How long do you think it will take"?

"At least a week, from the look of things", Sid assured him.

Webby wrote out a note, "Take this to the canteen manager and get him to put up enough food for at least 10 days, then you can take it with you". Sid was off like a shot, the canteen manager moaned a bit but there was nothing he could do but obey. Most of North Wales was at a standstill, and what was a few days food against that. While his order was being prepared, Sid nipped home to collect a couple of suitcases. Back at the canteen he watched with considerable satisfaction as into those cases went food in quality and quantity, the like of which Sid had not seen since 1939.

As he pushed these two back breaking suitcases onto the luggage rack of the Birkenhead Express, he could hear his old grandmother saying, "It's an ill wind that blows no one any good M'lad".

At Ruabon there was an engine and brake van from Bala waiting.

Sid loaded his precious suitcases of goodies and on the way he surveyed the the cab which would be his home for the next 10 days. It was a bit spartan, but Sid had slept many hours in worse places. He had a couple of blankets and a change of clothes, finding somewhere to wash would be simple. On arrival at Bala Sid contacted the foreman, "I shall want a driver for the plough, he needs to be a good man, someone who knows these roads around here and will not mind working overtime till this job is done".

The foreman didn't hesitate, "Got the very man for you, I'll send him over".

The Welshman climbed aboard a few minutes later. Sid followed him on to the footplate and said, "I'm Sid Clapham, Locomotive Inspector".

"Oh, are you", the Welshman replied, "You can call me 'Snow Plough', that's what they call me round here you see". They shook hands. Sid told him, "Call me Sid, that's what I have always been called, and I havn't seen any reason to change it yet".

The Welshman was mildly impressed, "What's the plan of campaign then Sid", he asked.

"Well", Sid began, sitting on the fireman's seat with one foot on the tender, "Our orders are to clear the line to Dolgellau first, and then the branch lines, how we do it is up to us. I'm not here to tell you that which you already know better, I'm here to make sure that nothing or nobody gets in our way while we're doing it".

'Snow Plough' was even more impressed but he still hadn't taken his coat off, or even removed his food bag from his shoulder.

It was after mid-day by now and 'Snow Plough' asked, "What do you propose we do today then".

Sid thought for a while, and choose his words carefully, "Let me put you in the picture further, I have the full authority of the Chief Superintendent to get this job done at any cost. Now I understand that you are the best man for the job around here, if you do your best for me, I'll do the same for you. I will do whatever is necessary to get these lines clear, I'll make the ruddy tea if that's what it takes, but remember, I may not know these roads or their problems like you do, but I didn't start on the railroad yesterday, and until the lines are cleared we have the say over anyone around here no matter who they are, so you tell me what you want and I'm here to see you get it". Sid held out his hand and the Welshman shook it.

"Feel happier now", Sid asked.

"Not really", 'Snow Plough' answered.

"What's yer problem", asked Sid.

"I don't like this tender engine on the plough, we usually have two tankys, and I think they are better".

"Well we had the tender engine to avoid unnecessary coaling and tank filling", Sid explained.

"Yes I know", came the reply, "But I don't see coal and water as being a problem, but two tankys are stronger than any tender engine, they have more acceleration and two lots of sand gear. Also, if the lead engine gets stuck with snow frozen around the brake blocks, or if it comes of the road, the second engine can pull it back on or go for assistance.

There are dozens of reasons why two tankys are better, and in any case we are used to them.

Sid considered this briefly, then said, "We'll have two tankys, I'll tell the foreman".

When Sid told the foreman, he clearly wasn't best pleased but he knew better than argue so out came the fitters to change the snow plough to the front of a 57 class tanky. A driver whose nick name was Boaty, came out with a second one to join them.

'Snow Plough' couldn't think when he had been more impressed or flattered and he now had his coat and jacket off and was fully committed.

"OK, what next", Sid asked.

"You get on to the permanent way inspector and get us a gang of platelayers, oh, and we shall need the breakdown vans and some coaches for the men and their tools. If you can arrange for them to be ready early tomorrow Sid, 'Boaty' and I will make sure that both these engines are in tip top shape, especially the sand tackle. Most important the sand tackle around here Sidney. I reckon it's too late to start tonight Sid, but leave it with us and we shall be ready at first light to knock the stuffing out of this job".

As Sid went off to do as he was told, 'Snow Plough' shouted after him, "Plenty of platelayers mind, there'll be a stack of bloody shovelling to do".

By the time Sid had fixed up for about 50 platelayers to accompany them plus the vans and coaches it was long past dark and he was wacked. He made his way to his van, made the fire up, put on the can for some tea then buttered some bread to have with a few slices of the canteen's boiled ham. He couldn't believe his luck as he gazed with great expectation at the suitcase of food. Not even the grocers of Bala themselves, would eat as well as Sidney Clapham this coming week. As he stretch out and closed his eyes, it was in the certain knowledge that he had been in many a worse situation.

Before first light he was crunching across frozen snow to the foreman's office. When he found the engines the two firemen were already there and Snow Plough and Boaty soon followed. Before it was fully light the two engines were coupled to the brake van and two eight wheelers. In the next two days they cleared the line and many sidings to Dolgelau. It had been an immensely fruitful two days with Sid clearing the way for the team to do their job. In the bright sunlight they had worked and bantered their way through.

Time and again it was necessary for Boatie to uncouple from the plough engine and stay with the coaches and platelayers while they cleared points and crossovers, or did emergency repairs while the plough went on with it's work. Each day confirmed the wisdom of changing the tender engine for two tankys. By the end of the fourth day every line was clear except the hazardous and precipitous branch to Blenau Festiniog. So far the new plough had performed perfectly.

At times they had run for miles at near passenger train speeds, with the snow lifting curling and arching away from the line in one single beautiful action which seemed almost too easy. Even so, the line to Festiniog was a different kettle of fish. The permanent way inspector had reported drifts of 10 feet in places, but even worse, underneath some of these was several inches of packed ice. The cycle of freezing nights, followed by warm midday sun, followed again by below zero temperatures had gradually formed many inches of ice some solid, some crystalized. This in turn had been covered time and again by fresh falls of snow. This situation constituted a completely unknown quantity.

by 10am on the first day, they had cleared several deep drifts with the plough. Then they come to the first badly blocked cutting. The line had been cut into the hillside by the men who had built it. As it curved around the hill, the steep rocky slope rose to the left, on their right only a small artificial embankment protected them from the steeply falling fields. The first drift on this hazardous stretch brought the plough with it's two engines to a shuddering stop, it was obvious that pack ice below the snow was responsible.

The platelayers piled out of the carriages and started shovelling like men possessed, throwing the loose snow over the low embankment and down into the valley. While they were shovelling Sid and the drivers rolled the engines back several hundred yards and secured the vans and coaches. Then they moved up to the obstruction again with just the two tankys and the plough. After much debate, it was decided that the platelayers would move most of the snow, and then knock holes in the ice about every 20 feet to give the plough a chance.

All this took several hours, time to watch the hill farmer struggling up the steep mountain side in efforts to reach his trapped sheep. He lifted several from the snow alive, only to see them kick feebly and die in his hands. They had been buried for several days. The newspapers reported that 20,000 had died in that one area, during that dreadful winter. "Snow Plough', not being one to stand about idle, decided to go to the farmers help. He climbed the fence only to disappear chest deep into a snow filled hole. His mates pulled him out to the accompaniment of cat calls and insults from the platelayers. Needless to say he didn't try it again.

It was mid-day by now and the ganger called Sid to assess the situation. The ice looked immovable and threatening but the ganger and his men had done all they could with the pick and shovel. To shift it all this way could take weeks, it would probably have melted first.

It was decision time for Sid and his drivers. He knew better than decide anything without consulting the drivers. The mutual respect which had built up over the past week or so was about to face it's most severe test.

Both drivers were chatting on the plough engine when Sid climbed aboard, "Well lads, it's up to us now", he stated simply. 'Snow plough' leaned on the regulator and stared thoughtfully into space. Boaty stared expectantly from one to the other.

"What do you suggest Sid"? asked Snow Plough.

"I think it's more important what you think", Sid replied, "You have more experience of this type of work than I, and in any case I am not going to ask you to do anything you are not comfortable with, you both know that the situation is pretty desperate, so what do ya think".

There are times in life when even the most artificially minded of men can see that the moment of truth has arrived, and this was just such a situation. All three men had considered the situation carefully, in fact they had thought of little else this last few hours, but now, it was time for action.

Boaty removed his pipe, "One things certain Sid, we shall not shift that lot with a gentle push".

"No you are right there", Snow Plough agreed.

"What do ya think will happen if we hit it really fast", Sid asked.

Boaty spoke, "I don't think it will pack up on us, this plough has always lifted the snow very quickly and thrown it clear even when the embankments are close in".

Snow Plough nodded in agreement.

All three men were silent for a moment then Sid spoke, "Of course that's true with snow but how about this ice"?

Snow Plough leaned forward and said deliberately, "Thats the million dollar question Sid and no sod on earth is going to answer that with any certainty because no one has ever seen conditions like this as long as there's been a railroad here, I can guarantee that".

"So what do we do"? asked Sid with an air of finality.

Snow Plough leaned forward again and asked, "Who's taking the rap if anything goes wrong Sid"? his question was mirrored in Boaty's eyes.

"Look", said Sid, sudden and loud, "What ever you chaps decide, you will have my full backing and I will take responsibility, and there's no way that I shall ever go back on that, understand? not ever".

The two Welshmen were impressed. In the Black Country such talk would have seemed a bit over the top, but not here, the Welshmen liked a bit of drama, and they also liked to know where they stood, and Sid had just given them both.

Boaty moved to go back to his engine, before he did Sid had one last question, "How fast are we going in"? he asked.

Snow Plough looked at Boaty, "As fast as we bloody well can I say, shit or bust, isn't it.

Boaty just nodded and started walking back to his engine.

While he did, there was just one more question in Snow Plough's eyes,

"Do you want to climb down Sid, there's no sense in us all taking a risk is there".

"Not bloody likely", Sid assured him, "We are in this together, besides why should you have all the fun".

Snow Plough raised his eyebrows just slightly, in approval. Boaty was now back on his engine and ready to go.

The two tankys moved slowly back to get a good run, at the end of the run they stopped and the two drivers swung their levers into forward gear with a decisive bang. All the way back Snow Plough had had his sand lever open and now the line in front was nicely brown with fresh dry sand.

The whole valley seemed to fall silent, the platelayers were lighting their fags and staring expectantly, their shirts steaming in the sun, they knew that they were about to witness something a bit special. Over three hundred yards of clear sand covered line lay between the tanky's and the ominous great stretch of snow and ice. From where they stood, it seemed to assume a menacing threat that hadn't been obvious at close quarters.

On their left the snow covered mountain rose steeply. To their right, the glistening white slope tobogganed down into the valley. With the sun shining from a clear blue sky, it was an incredibly beautiful and unforgettable scene.

A scene set for triumph or disaster?.

Sid pushed the second alternative firmly from his mind. Whatever the result might be, these next few moments would be frozen in Sid's mind for ever.

He stood half outside the cab and his eyes level with the cab roof. The driver opened the regulator and the two engines moved forward, the second engine slipped for a second, it's exhaust roar echoing around the hill sides and sending a thick black column of steam and smoke high into the cloudless sky. Immediately, she gripped again and the two engines began to beat in unison, the beats quickly became a bark and then a roar and finally a deafening rattling crescendo as the two tanky's shook in every plate and rivet at the incredible demand on their power as they hurled 80 tons of solid steel at that snow and ice.

In the last few yards the ice pack literally streaked at them. As they hit, there was the most massive bonecrunching thud. To Sid it seemed as if they stood still for an instant, of course they couldn't have, but in that awesome instant of collision, the shape that the engineers had built into that plough was tested to the limit.

Only the incredible shutter speed of the human memory could could freeze that moment when steel hit ice. Open mouthed platelayers knee deep in snow; the ice; the snow covered rocks; the brilliant blue sky; the whole incredible scene was engraved in Sid's brain by excitement and fear.

One micro second after they struck and and the snow in front of them rose, lifting, cracking and glistening like the bow wave of an ocean liner.

Another second and a great cascade of gleaming ice was shooting into the crisp clear air cleaving away against the blue sky like a giant breathtaking fountain.

Yet another second and the gleaming glittering crackling arch was complete.

It was sustained for moment after moment, an immense moving shimmering monument, one foot embedded in the bow wave which rose continuously before them and the other breaking and thudding and rolling down the snowy mountain side.

For second on second the shimmering streaking arch sent ice rocketing on a giant curve into the valley. 200 men watched in breathless silence and then it was gone.

And gone with it was the 300 yard mass of ice and snow which only seconds before had seemed so threatening.

200 hats flew in the air and 200 voices rang out across the valley as the platelayers roared their approval. The two drivers tried to stop the rocketing tanky's, but to no avail. Snow and ice had frozen to the brake blocks and the brakes were useless. On down the line they went, hurling snow and ice aside until, almost spent, they came to rest against the next deeply blocked section of line.

Sid breathed deep of the pure mountain air, suddenly it was a wonderful day, they had found the answer, courage and determination had won through. There were handshakes and quiet smiles all round, sealing the moment of relief. They stared back at nearly a quarter of a mile of clear track, was it only seconds ago that the ice had stood impassively, daring them to move against it.

There was still plenty of work to do before they would steam triumphantly into Blenau Festiniog. In total, Sid would spend twelve long days in the Welsh hills before the job was done. Twelve days of bantering and laughing with those Welsh railroad men. Every day a day of sweet achievement carried out with great pleasure in the gradually warming sun of a long awaited Welsh spring. Sid slept every night in the Guards van, he had plenty of coal to keep the stove pipe red hot against the freezing night, and more than sufficient food. In fact he had been warmer and more comfortable than half the population of the British Isles.

When the time had come to leave, he was not short of a friendly hand to shake, his departure was a damn sight more cheerful than his arrival had been, nearly a fortnight before.

He settled back in the compartment of the stopper on his way back to W'ton with a feeling of deep contentment. On Bala platform behind him, he had just left more than a dozen Welshmen who had broken their sleep to see him off.

It had been warm handshakes and best wishes from men who would never forget Sid, as he would never forget them. They had accomplished a task of National importance, and more perhaps than that, they had helped to ease the lives of countless folk of the small Welsh towns and villages, of the hill farmer on whom we all depended. He had arrived in an atmosphere of mistrust and depression and turned it into one of friendship and confidence.

As he settled back into the plush seats of the first class carriage, He saw himself as a child in the back streets of Whitmore Reans W'ton, and now he was a Locomotive inspector, no less, a trouble shooter, he was a friend and protector of all Loco men, and only rarely and reluctantly their prosecutor.

A man at the peak of his powers and experience, every day brought a different job, a new challenge. At that moment, Sid Clapham wouldn't have changed place's with anyone else on earth.

A WINDY NIGHT ON THE CREWE BRANCH

"G" climbed the bank to Oxley shed. He was feeling more than a little fragile. It was 2 am and he had just come from a party where there had been plenty to eat and drink. This coupled with a chronic shortage of sleep had produced a number of unpleasant sensations so familiar to all young firemen. The quaking knee, the throbbing head, the sleep-heavy eyes were all the lot of every fireman who over indulged on night shift (were there any who didn't?).

G had a particularly bad attack on this occasion because he'd been a little indiscreet all the week. His job was to work a special to Crewe then bring the engine back to Oxley. When he was feeling fit this would have seemed a nice little trip out, but in his present state it was as daunting as a trip up the Amazon in a leaky canoe. To add to his pains, he was paired with a bloke who had no sense of humour and never over indulged or anything of that sort and 'couldn't understand any fool who did'. He was not a bad mate really, but was sickeningly fit and ready for work at any hour of the day or night and expected everyone else to be the same. If they weren't he could be very testy indeed. So G was not expecting a lot of sympathy from this direction and he wasn't to be disappointed.

He booked on and located the 28'er which he now had less than an hour to prepare. His mate was already at work; sleeves rolled back, his big mitts wiping away at the feeders and oil bottles with enough gusto for ten men. G shambled up, feeling more weary and wracked with pain every passing minute. "Okay mate", he mumbled with a hint of a whimper designed to provoke some compassion. His mate who we shall call 'Frosty' for frosty he was looked at G as one looks at something rather unpleasant such as a blocked drain or the like.

"Bin on the pop, 'ave we?" he remarked as he turned and walked to the front of the engine. G climbed wearily onto the footplate; it was cold and sooty, smoke billowed from around the firehole doors. There was hardly enough steam to work the blower, most of the tools were missing and on the tender, massive lumps of coal balanced precariously one on another in a most threatening manner. He felt faint at the sight of it all.

Never fear though G, help was at hand. In the cabin with no immediate job was one of G's drinking companions. He had just risen from a couple of hour's of delicious stolen sleep. He was now refreshed, full of energy and ready for work. Still without a job, he had thought of G.

In just a few moments he was climbing aboard the 28'er with almost as much gusto as Frosty.

"How ya doin', G, yer drunken old sod?" were his first words. "Do ya want a bit of help, you debauched old bugger you".

G ignored the flattery. "Oh Christ, I'll say I do!" he yelled.

"Go and get some sand and trim the lamps then, while I get on with this lot", ordered the Good Samaritan and G responded like a shot.

The Good Samaritan soon had the fire spread across the firebars. Cracking up coal like a man possessed, he gradually fed the smaller lumps to the flames. As the steam pressure rose, he worked faster and faster breaking the coal, feeding the fire, swilling the footplate, damping down the dust and wiping the sooty controls with an oily rag. One job to another and back again until the whole footplate had become a clean, warm, friendly, living place. With fifteen minutes left to go, G climbed back onto the footplate to see the clean, orderly ship-shape conditions that his Good Samaritan had created.

"Thanks a lot mate," said G with some feeling.

"That's okay G," replied the good Samaritan, "I'll see you some time" and he was gone, leaving G in much better shape.

Frosty climbed aboard and moved the engine out to the water column. He looked quite pleased at the sight of the tidy footplate. As they moved out of the shed, the cool night air wafted around G's face and he felt decidedly better. At the column he grasped the chain and pulled the great arm around until the huge leather 'bag' was sliding into the gaping black hole of the tank. Frosty turned the valve on full and a torrent of water gushed and bubbled; it was a most refreshing sound. With the tank full, he clambered down onto the footplate to hear Frosty shout "Bring her over the points, mate." G took the hand-brake off and moved the massive loco slowly back. As it cleared the points, he saw Frosty pull the points over and call him forward with a wave of his arm. Frosty climbed aboard and took hold of the regulator as they moved slowly up the rise into Oxley North sidings. They stood under the signal box for about ten minutes or so then the shunter called them back onto the train. Frosty stood chatting to the guard and shunter as they hooked on and were ready to leave on time.

The 28'er screeched and creaked it's way out of the sidings and onto the main line. As they approached the canal viaduct, G could see the guard's white light swing 45 wagons back; it indicated that the train was complete and on the move. G waved the gauge lamp in reply, "Right away mate," he shouted. Frosty nodded and gradually urged the engine on until all the couplings were tight and they were on their way.

G felt mightily relieved by now, for he had heard the guard say that the train was something special and they would be getting a straight run through to Crewe. He reckoned he could easily keep his eyes open that long, then bringing the engine back would be a doddle.
Besides that, he knew that once at Crewe, the foreman there would probably decide to hang onto the engine and send them home on the first passenger. G could already feel the soft seats of the first passenger train yielding to his tired limbs. Oh, the sweetness of that stolen sleep. It most certainly is a crass and stupid thing to dance and booze the night away when you know you're on the early shift. But who but the crass and the stupid can know the ecstasy of closing the bloodshot eye and giving way at last to Mother Nature's most compelling appeal.

However, G had to get to Crewe first and they were now bowling nicely through Codsall and apart from a throbbing head and a few gripey pains in his tummy, he was quite well; which, in view of his recent foolishness, was very encouraging. With all the sticks off, the 28'er was soon hammering its' way up Shifnal Bank and G was finding the pains in his bread-basket getting worse again. By the time they were passing Madeley Junction, even Frosty could see that he was struggling.

"What's the trouble?" shouted Frosty above the barking of the 28'er.

"Bloody guts-ache," G shouted back, shaking his head in annoyance and pain.

"Get over here", barked Frosty. This meant that he would take over the firing while G stood on the driver's side watching for signals and obeying instructions in handling the loco. Frosty was not really a hard man and he certainly didn't have to stretch himself to fire and drive if needed, but he was fed up to the back teeth with firemen who went without sleep and on the booze. He'd never done it himself and he objected to carrying the can when others did.

His manner was irritable and off hand as they rolled down the bank towards Ketley junction. He pulled the hand-brake on to close the train together in case of a hold up at Wellington. Suddenly G let out a cry of pain and doubled up over the lever in the driver's corner.

"What's up?" yelled Frosty.

G just shook his head slowly from side to side. Frosty walked over. One look was enough to see that G was in real trouble, his face was ashen and contorted in pain.

Frosty almost had to drag him across the footplate in order to make room to control the engine. He could see all the sticks were off through Wellington but he brought the train under control then hurriedly wrote a message in his log book and ripped out the page. He then wrapped it around a small piece of coal in readiness to throw it off passing the Box at Wellington. Frosty had made a rapid decision in those fleeting seconds. Realising that it was too late to stop in the platform at Wellington, he calculated that the nearest and best place to ask for an ambulance would be Hodnet. Even with years of hindsight, there's no doubt that he was exactly right. So he attracted the signalman's attention by blowing a couple of 'crows' on the whistle.

The signalman was out of the box and picking up the note in seconds. Frosty and G were picking up speed across the junction and away down the bank to Crudgington. G was no better, doubled up with pain he just shook his head in confusion when spoken to. Frosty was busy as he approached and passed Crudgington. He nipped smartly from side to side, dealing with the train as the line dipped by the distant signal and again in Crudgington itself. He caught just a few words from the 'Bobby' as they passed the box in a roar of exhaust. It seemed the ambulance would be waiting in Hodnet platform.

They climbed the gentle rise beyond Crudgington and were running light and free across the flat heron country surrounding the winding river Tern when it happened. G's poor distended, pain wracked tummy could stand NO MORE and he broke wind. It started as a sort of strangled whine that had Frosty looking for trouble with the engine and gradually rose in volume in a most alarming fashion, drowning out the rattle of the engine completely at one point. It held both men transfixed by wide eyed wonder and curiosity, unable to credit their hearing; astonished and baffled by its' power. Stories that the guard, 45 clattering wagons back, rushed out of his cab in a panic are, of course, wild exaggeration.

Nevertheless, there is NO doubt at all that this was something extraordinary by way of a fart. The volume was frightening and bewildering, as much for the victim as for his mate. It was said that such a long sustained note would have brought a flush of pride to the face of Eddie Calvert! We can assume from all accounts that if records of such things were kept, this could well have been a world beater.

G's expression of fear and pain passed gently through astonishment and disbelief into one of sheer bliss as the agony of distension slowly faded; leaving a calm relief, the likes of which is rarely experienced by man. His mate's open mouthed amazement now turned to amusement. Even this dour man had the suggestion of a smile on his lips, you had to look closely, though. G slumped in the corner.

"Oh, thank God for that." he said from the bottom of his heart. His pale face told of peace after great pain, it required no words. It was a picture that was clear even to his unsympathetic and unimaginative mate. Frosty looked across at G, in between glances in the direction of the distant signal for Hodnet. He seemed indulgent and slightly amused at the whole alarming, but now quite harmless, experience.

But this uncharacteristic mood of his only lasted a brief moment or two and faded rapidly as the thought of ambulances, possible police, of explanations all awaiting him at Hodnet, and later, Official Reports!

"You mean to tell me that you've caused all this aggro' for the sake of a good fart?" he hooted, deliberately belittling the event in his anger.

"Well I was in agony mate," appealed G. "I had no idea what it was, it's never happened before". "Never happened before?" came the reply in a nasty, mocking voice. "I shouldn't think it has happened before, you effing great pillock.
I hope you're going to explain to that mob at Hodnet and answer a few reports. I hope you'll tell them that you stopped an important goods train and alerted half of Shropshire at the dead of night all for a touch of the wind."

Well, to describe this 'happening' as a touch of the wind was, of course, the understatement of the century and it was he and not his mate who was going to be faced with explanations. But he was in no mood to speak of logic and so he gave G a continuous tongue lashing until they were pulling up to the signal box at Hodnet.

The signalman was leaning out of the box. He began to shout "There's an ambulance on the platform and a relief fireman on his way. If you pull . . ".

Frosty waited no longer, "We don't need them," he shouted. "Pull the sticks off." The Bobby was astonished and began to splutter about "ambulances and . ."

"Pull the bloody sticks off!" bellowed Frosty face and the startled signalman obeyed. The starting signal turned green and Frosty opened the regulator wide. The engine began to cough then bark and roar as it gathered speed towards the platform and bridge. There was just a suggestion of light in the sky as the ambulancemen, stretcher at the ready, stood waiting. And it was with complete amazement that they watched the train gathering speed and passing them with a deafening roar; the fireman standing looking at them with a slightly baffled look on his face. G was rather glad of this for he had not looked forward to explaining to the ambulance crew the reasons they were no longer needed.

Frosty's sudden and abrupt departure was ignorant and bad-mannered, that's for sure, but it also had a touch of inspiration and decisiveness about it. For in seconds the blasting engine smothered the bridgehole and platform in steam and smoke and Hodnet disappeared from view and glad G was for it. His relief from pain was ample compensation for the irritated contempt with which his mate treated him throughout the rest of the night. Frosty ignored or avoided all questions at Crewe and again on arrival back at Oxley and never even said 'Ta ra mate' to G when he left. He would no doubt have to make a report about it all eventually, giving satisfactory explanations of such unusual conduct.

We shall never know what was written there. Knowing the man, he could have invented a short, plausible lie, or on the other hand, he could have told the unvarnished truth in old English terms, he was quite capable of either. In any case, it would have made amusing reading to anyone in possession of the truth, I'm sure. We shall never know now for it went the way of all these reports, no doubt. I often think if only we knew the true stories behind all those 'Fairy' stories known as enginemen's special reports, what a rich and amusing source of information would be tapped and what a marvellous insight we would have into the difficulties and dangers of the footplate and not least, the native ingenuity of enginemen in explaining the unexplainable.

TRAUMA AT OXLEY

It was almost 2am, there was no moon but it was a mild and pleasant night. Jack and I walked and talked our way past Oxley coal stage. Jack was my Driver and I was his Fireman, we spent more time together than with any other persons, 8 to 12 hours most days.

Jack knew something about almost everything, we were great mates, always talking on every subject under the sun. The foreman at Stafford rd had said, "Jack, you and your mate go down to Oxley will yer, George Holland needs a set of men. I don't know what for".

George was the shed foreman at Oxley and the job could be anything from a coal train to a fast parcels we weren't bothered either way.

I was recently married and with a young beautiful and happy wife at home and Jack to share my working hours, every day was enjoyment and fulfilment. I remember that as we approached the shed office we were laughing about something.

Then I spotted him over Jacks shoulder, the dark figure of a big man leaping frantically over the double track to our right. As he came into the light of the gas lamp I recognised him as one of the shunters from Oxley North sidings, he came nearer and I could see his face was pale and his manner frantic, it boded ill on the railroad did that.

"Are either of you, first aid blokes?", he asked anxiously.

Well I had taken a first aid course the year I left school while I was a messenger with the ARP, and I had taken another about 1943 while in the Home Guard. I hadn't finished either and I had never taken an exam but I could recall some of it and still considered myself to be a first aider of sorts.

"I know a bit", I replied.

"Go on over the sidings then the under shunter has been knocked down on the crossing, his legs are off I rekon".

I felt a cold hand grasp me tightly around the middle and my legs didn't feel as solid as they had a moment ago but I knew I had to go.

"Come on Jack", I said. To my amazement Jack leaned against the wall, his face ashen in the gas light and said, "I can't go mate, I couldn't do anything if I did.. You go".

Jack who was ice cool in any situation on the footplate, was beaten by the thought of blood

I moved off and as I jumped the rails the shunter caught me up shouting, "Grab this mate", I grabbed one end of the rolled up stretcher and walked in front over the pitch black 50 foot or so of rough banks which lay between the shed and the sidings.

We found the 3 foot gap between the buildings and walked through into the lights of Oxley sidings. To our right, where the railroads fanned out and criss crossed, we could see half a dozen men around the prone figure of the under shunter, he was lying across the rails.

Three of them were supporting his head and shoulders while one brave soul kneeled with rolled up sleeves binding the mangled legs. As we drew nearer I recognised the Guard who was binding the lads legs and he recognised me,

"Worro Geoff lad", he said as I placed the stretcher on the rails beside the injured lad.

"Worro Fred", I answered. Fred was a first world war veteran and he talked confidently and cheerfully while he worked.

The waggons had crushed 4 inches of flesh and bone to pulp and Fred had already bound the stumps firmly and he was now folding over the few inches of ankle and foot which still adhered to them, binding them loosely to the legs. The soles of his boots looked up towards his face and the feet flopped over crazily.

Fred organised four men to lift the injured lad while he held the poor mangled legs. As they lifted, others slid the stretcher underneath. The lad cried out for a moment, and then he was laid on the stretcher. As we covered him with blankets I saw at close quarters his empty desperate eyes in a waxen face and his flesh hanging from the stretcher in ribbons.

Someone else grabbed the head of the stretcher thank goodness, I doubted whether my legs would have lifted him. Fred went to wash the blood from his hands. Six pairs of hands helped with the stretcher and two men shone the inadequate oil lamps onto the ground as we made our way back the way we had come, bumping and jarring over the rough ground in the inky blackness.

From then on, I knew I should have taken charge, slowed them down, gone more smoothly while I held his shoulders and spoke to him, encouraged him, but I did non of these things. I was too shaken, too shocked, I just helped to support one side of the stretcher and somehow the helpers ignored my feeble attempts to give orders as they rushed head long towards the shed where the wheels stood which were the only way of moving a stretcher around the shed. The Ambulance was already standing 200 yds away at the top of the bank, that was the nearest it could get. The stretcher was dropped roughly on to this wheel cart, for it was nothing else, and as they turned in the direction of the ambulance the foreman told me that a Chester train was awaiting me at the Branch junction and Jack and I left.

I didn't sleep much the next day. A thousand times I saw that lads waxen face as every jolt and every panicky shout drove him deeper into shock, but worst of all was the question. 'If Fred hadn't have been there, would I have failed him completely?'. I hadn't done enough, I knew that, nerves had beaten me and now guilt and shame twisted my insides.

When we booked on next night we learned that the lads wife had been at his bedside when he came out of the anesthetic. He was distraught because his legs had gone, she had tried desperately to convince him that her love would pull him through, but he just turned his face away and died.

My feelings of Guilt and shame increased, I see now that for a young lad of 24 with no previous experience to think that he should have coped properly with such a situation was pure silly arrogance, and what ever I had done, he may still have died, but it made no difference then and it makes little difference now. I hadn't done what I had been trained to do and that may have cost him his life. Strangely enough I didn't think any the worse of Jack who hadn't felt able to help at all, but nothing could change my feelings about myself. It has always been there to add to the load of guilt which many of us carry around with us day by day.

The intense pain brought on by shame and guilt did ease gradually, but it never left me, it went on year after year, it was still there when I was thirty, forty , fifty. When I was sixty I tried to look back squarely at the 24 year old stranger that was me, and forgive him as I certainly would have done for anyone else,.. but I couldn't,....and I don't suppose I ever will.

INTER CITY

Many people may wonder what it is like to take a trip to London on a Castle or a King. Well the following is from my memory of events of the early 1950's.

We book on for the Inter City Express just before 4pm. The Castle is waiting, the men who have prepared her are washing their hands and telling us the state of the fire and tender etc. It is a beautiful spring afternoon as we roll quietly up to the shed Signal. In about 2 minutes it comes off and we travel smoothly up the slight bank to Wolverhampton Low Level with the safety valve blowing off steam. This is to lower the water level allowing us to keep her quiet in the station. After another few minutes of waiting I put the injector on as we back on to the train and I then drop down on the drivers side and walk to the back to hook on. Ducking under the buffers and grabbing the engine coupling, I see that all my bits and pieces are clear then shout "Ease up!".

The driver opens the regulator with appropriate force and the engine heaves against the carriage buffers allowing me to drop the shackle over the carriage hook. "OK" I shout and my mate eases off tightening the coupling with the buffers still slightly depressed.

Back on the footplate I switch off the injector because the boiler is almost full now. We are waiting for the Guards 'Right Away' hoping that it comes before the engine begins to blow off steam again deafening everyone around. Sure enough I see the green flag waving 12 carriages down the platform and shout "Right away mate". The driver opens the regulator with a calculated tug and awaits the result. The engine and train begin to move, gently at first and then gathering speed as we approach the tunnel. I watch the coaches leaving the platform until I'm sure that all is well and the train is following and then get up the corner for the trip through the tunnel.

It's not a long tunnel but it does fitt the engine very closely and despite the need to get the train moving the driver usually throttles down to avoid choking us both as the steam and smoke billow into the cab. Out into the bright sunshine again the smoke and steam quickly clear to reveal that we are in a deep cutting, this quickly gives way to more open surroundings as we pass Monmore Green Greyhound stadium and Stow Heath Signal box. My mate, Jack, Shuts off for a few seconds to run round the tight curve of Priestfield Junction and platforms at no more than 30mph.

Once around these he picks them up again and hammers them up to about 50 miles per hour as we pass Bilston Station. Half way between there and Wednesbury he shuts off again to comply with the 35 mile per hour limit around the sharp bend starting in Wednesbury station. Once clear of Wednesbury station, the driver gives her the first real push as he tries to raise the speed up West Bromich Bank.

I start to fire the engine for the first time here. Care is needed as the 18" of fire which the engine preparer has provided is not yet fully burnt through. I fling a shovel full or two down the front end where the fire seems to be flaming through and make sure that the back corners are full. The engine is working heavily now all the way through Swan Village and West Bromich and begins to pick up speed very quickly once we are over top of the bank. I have the firebox doors open now, despite the fact that the clock (steam gauge) has gone back coming up the bank I have at least 5 minutes to keep her quiet in Snow Hill so I need to leave room in the boiler to enable me to keep the injectors on while standing in the platform. The driver gives her the first real run of the journey down through Handsworth and Queens Head we reach about 65 mph. We slow down again as the line curves first this way then that through the crowded built up areas of Winson Green and Hockley and finally under the bridges into Birmingham Snow Hill.

I put the injector on. We shall soon see whether I have left enough room in the boiler or have over done it, in which case we shall have to leave Snow Hill with less than a boiler full of water.

The big clock on the platform is showing 4/54pm we have 6 minutes to kill. The run from Wolverhampton has just been like a leg stretcher for the big engine but now we start the real work of the trip which won't end until the driver shuts off for Paddington. There's a feel of excitement just below the surface, despite the fact that I have done this quite a few times before, and the driver many many times before, it still holds a certain thrill because the coming journey is not a cut and dried event, it will depend on me and my mate doing our jobs right, whether the engine is up to it, whether the coal is of decent quality and a number of other things all of which are about to be tested to the limit.

As the big station clock moves towards the upright position of 5pm I begin to keep my eyes fixed on the place 12 carriages back where the guard will wave his green flag any moment. Every second assumes an importance out of all proportion to it's normal value because the timing between here and Leamington leaves nothing to spare. As the clock hits the 12 so the Guard waves his flag and I give the driver "Right Away mate". He lifts the regulator and we move slowly at first out of the platform and into the tunnel.

Despite the tunnel the driver doesn't ease up now, he pushes the engine on and we are blasted with steam and smoke as we enter the tunnel, but we have no need to worry, the tunnel has a steep incline which means that we can pick up speed very quickly, this is just as well, because we need all the help we can get to to keep time between here and Leamington. We leave the tunnel at about 50 miles per hour, the steep slope of the tunnel has given us a flying start. Out on to Bordesley Viaduct we go streaking across the house and factory tops of a crowded Birmingham. In seconds we fly through Bordesely Station gathering speed with every beat of the engine. The fire is beginning to break up now into a white hot inferno into which the black un-burned coal is shrinking fast. I start to fire along the centre of the box. This keeps the sides of the fire box mainly free of coal.

As the roaring beats of he engine and the vibration grow so the partly burned coal fall into the raging fire on each side. By directing a stream of air down the box with the shovel it is possible to keep watch on how the coal is burning. There is about 18" of solid fire developing now and it is essential to keep it up without ever 'over doing' it or blocking the back of the brick arch. In between firing I shall be helping the driver by watching for the signals which appear first on my side. I shall also be using the pet pipe to wet the coal down to avoid the dust and keep the small coal which escapes the shovel from becoming a hazard by using the hand brush to keep the footplate clear.

From now on it will be shovel, pet pipe, hand brush most of the way to London. Both my mate and I know every bridge which goes under or over the railway, every platform and every signal. Each cutting and embankment is so familiar that we know where we are most of the time blindfold.

Although we are now travelling at more than 65 miles per hour the speed seems much faster because through Small Heath, Tyseley and Ackocks Green the bridges, platforms and signals are all so close that we appear to be flying. Once through Olton the buildings begin to disappear in favour of open countryside and our real speed begins to build up. Soon we are doing 75 miles an hour and still increasing Solihull Widney Manor, Knowle and Dorridge pass us at increasing speed. We are holding our own nicely, the fire is maintaining steam with the exhaust injector keeping the water level up and I'm beginning to enjoy the trip immensely.

We hurtle through Lapworth at just over 80 mph, we are doing so well that I have time to lean out the drivers side to wave to the signalman in Lapworth box. We saw him several nights last week on a night goods train. In less than a minute we are approaching the water troughs at Rowington. The method of filling the tank at the troughs consists of lowering a scoop into the small canal formed by the troughs; the force of the engines forward motion forces the water into the scoop and up the duct which rises diagonally up to the mushroom on the back of the tender where it is turned back into the tank.

If the fireman gets this right, the partly empty tank will be filled in seconds, if he fails to get it right he either; fails to fill the tank at all in which case the train may be forced to stop for water; or, the scoop stays down and the tank overflows with shocking consequences such as the water pouring onto the footplate bringing coal with it. In a bad case this can fill the footplate with coal and send coal and water cascadeing through the gangway onto the track.

The two factors which drastically effect this process are first; the easy movement of the scoop operating gear, this means oiling all moving parts before leaving the shed, and secondly; the correct use of the scoop, as the scoop is lowered the water enters it at the front but leaves at the back where it is hinged on to the shoot. As the scoop lowers so the gap at the back closes. Until the gap is almost closed the amount of water entering the tank is minimal, but the trick is, not to let the gap close completely because the moment it does the entire force of the water is concentrated on the front end of the scoop and it is almost impossible to raise it until the end of the troughs is reached.

So it is matter of judgement which comes with time to keep the scoop just clear of it's lowest position and to raise it before the water gauge reaches the top.

In this case we have no trouble, I just move behind the driver as we approach the troughs I begin to lower the scoop until I feel the grip of the water and then with the handle in the crook of one arm I just ease it back up or drop it down a fraction while watching the gauge carefully.

With that done I resume the routine of firing, watering the coal and sweeping the footplate as we pass Hatton station and down the bank at 80 mph plus, through Warwick down into the dip where the line goes under the road bridges and over the river Avon, then finally up into Leamington where we draw to a stand in the platform.

Leamington is an essential stopping place from the point of view of the passengers, but from the point of view of the crew working an express passenger train it could not be worse. It stops the train in full flight just at the foot of a long rising incline. It is always a disappointment to have to stop in such a place but nearly all London trains do so. We get used to it, after all, the train is run for passengers not the crew.

All the way down the bank I have been once again involved in trying to leave a little room in the boiler to 'keep her quiet' at Leamington but still have a full boiler and plenty of steam on leaving.

Today we are lucky and it all seems so easy, once we leave Leamington we are non-stop to Paddington. Soon the green flag waves and we pull out of the platform. There is little room for the driver to nurse her now. The next 10 miles or so are hard against the collar and there is only one way to get them on the move and that is to push the regulator right across and gradually wind the lever back as we increase speed. The big engine responds like a giant. In a few minutes the driver has been able to pull the lever well back but she is still roaring like a lion as she hauls the twelve eight wheelers up to about 50 miles per hour. If we can keep her on the 'mark' (Blow off point on the steam gauge), we shall increase or hold our speed all the way through Fenny Compton.

I begin to fire the engine again almost as soon as we clear the signals at Leamington. The fire is roaring and crumbling now and only a constant feed of coal can stop us from losing fire. It is useless to pile coal on coal so I have to fire about four or five shovels at a time giving each lot time to begin burning before feeding in the next, all the time watching for that assuring puff of smoke which mean that the fire is burning well.

We are so busy now that the miles fly by, Foss Road goes by in a flash with it's wide open spaces and we are soon into the cutting which leads to the short tunnel before Harbury. Into the cutting we go with the big engine blasting and echoing off the tree lined embankment.

Despite having the exhaust injector on we are still almost on the mark and the water has only just started to come down. My mate, Jack, smiles at this because he likes a fast run and he knows that I do too, so if the opportunity arises we will have the steam and water to 'let her rip'. We blast our way through the tunnel and through Harbury and in seconds are running through Greaves's sidings where the buildings including the houses of the workers are thickly coated with the dust of the cement works which dominates this depot. We move a little faster thought Greaves's because the gradient eases a little but it soon goes against the collar again as we hammer our way on towards Fenny Compton. Once through there we will not be long before the gradient starts to ease completely.

As we approach Fenny Compton I have a good look into the firebox because I have noticed that the unburnt coal is building up at the back end of the arch. This can't be allowed to continue because if I can't pass that and feed the front end of the box, which by the way is nearly 14" from the fire hole, the fire will soon burn in holes and the cold air will cause the clock to fall like a stone. I must use the fire irons, so I grab the long pricker which is a one inch hooked bar which will reach to the front of the box if need be, and with a quick look at Jack, who nodds to indicate that there are no bridges or other obstructions flying our way I lift the pricker up high over the cab and swing it down and straight into the fire hole.

As I push the unburnt coal forward to clear the back end of the arch Jack shouts, "That shifted something mate". Which means that clouds of black smoke are shooting out of the chimney, proving that the strategy was exactly right. As I draw the pricker back I gently ease the fire to loose a little air in and by the time the pricker comes out it is red hot for 18" of it's length and sparkling white hot at the tip. I look at Jack again and he nodds again and I heave the big bar over the top and back into the rack. By the time this has been done and I have fired her again, watered the coal and tidied up we are flying through Claydon Crossing and Cropredy at more than 70 mph.

It all seems so easy now because we are still doing well for steam and water and making up time as well. It's often like this because they don't put the crocks or the bad coal on the London jobs usually, but it can be different, Oh dear me it can, there arc times when we have had to shut off and free wheel after Cropredy to get a bit of steam and water back but lets not think of that now eh. At Banbury Ironstone, where the ironstone is mined and transported to the big blast furnaces at Bilston, Jack shuts off. This is because there is a 60 mph check though the platforms at Banbury. As we approach the Junction the signals are on anyway, we both begin to say some naughty words because after all that hammering up the bank there is no way that we want to stop and have to start it all over again.

We are only cursing in light jocular manner yet because we think that as we approach, and before we really slow down, the 'Bobby' will pull the sticks off.

When this doesn't happen the swearing takes on a more serious nature altogether, and we begin to say such silly thing as, "What the hell does he think he's * + * * doing". And, "All the time in the world and he's got to stop us in full * * + * * flight", all completely fruitless because what ever we say will make no difference. The sticks stay on and after the excitement of the chase we gradual come to a stand and the world becomes strangely quiet. Not for long though, that fire which has been sustaining steam and water against all that hard work doesn't take long to fill the boiler and the safety valve lifts to deafen everyone within miles.

We can see the signalman miming indecipherable messages to us so we are in no doubt that he knows we are waiting and that he is trying to get the road for us. He's clearly upset at stopping us and we are pretty sure that he has let someone out on the clear understanding that they wouldn't stop us, Oh gullible fool, now they have stopped us and he will have to explain why he didn't keep, who ever it was, inside until after we had gone. Our amazement and annoyance grow rapidly as the time ticks by. The engine is making a noise that surely can be heard at Paddington and the passengers are staring out as if they are expecting us to explode any moment.

On occasions such as this a minute seems like an hour, our disbelief and the Bobby's anxiety is growing with every second.

Unbelievably we are standing there 12 minutes before the sticks finally come off and as we pass the box the Bobby comes to the window and spreads his arms and shows us a face full of the most intense frustration and we make it even worse by nodding and tutting to show our complete contempt for every one on the railroad except us. As we gather speed again Jack asks,

"Shall we try to make it up mate?" He loves a fast run does Jack.

I enjoy it as much as Jack when the engine is right so I say, "Arr, go for it Jack".

Jack doesn't need any more encouragement than that and he puts the regulator right across to set the Castle roaring into those coaches and increasing speed rapidly. I don't have much time to see anything for a minute or two because the 12 minutes standing at Banbury has allowed the fire to burn right through and I have to get on top of it again. By the time I have done that we are flying towards the troughs at King Sutton.

It couldn't be easier to pick up water, if we have this engine all the week it will be a doddle. Once again I stand behind Jack to lower the scoop and watch the water gauge, as soon as I feel the snatch of the scoop I pull it back or lower it down according to how fast or slow the gauge is rising. It takes only seconds to fill the tank and the scoop is secure again and we are streaking towards Aynho Junction at 70 mph, despite the facing points and the long curve we go round with only a few sudden but controlled swings as the bogies pull her round the bend. Once on the straight Jack lifts the regulator and the big engine roars into life to rocket up the bank.

I am working as hard now, as I will be at any time on the journey. I'm trying to maintain a good fire while the engine tries to pull the fire to bits. Only for a short time though, after hammering our way through the cutting and the short tunnel before Ardley Jack starts to gradually ease the regulator and slowly pull the lever back as we pick up speed. Next I spot the distant signal for Bicester and give Jack the 'Right Away'. The steam gauge went back a bit coming up the bank through Ardley but now its back on the mark with the safety valve just fizzing. This is the very ideal that we always aim at but not too often achieve. Oh, we achieve it with ease in the cabin when we are spare and shooting a line, we achieve it so easily and regularly that it seems more or less the norm, but on the footplate flying towards the distant for Bicester, perhaps, not quite so often.

Never the less we are doing it now and Jack and I are really enjoying it. The Castle speedo show 80 miles per hour passing the distant and 85 before we reach Bicester platform. By the time we approach the platform we have exceeded 90 mph and the passengers waiting for the stopper stand staring in un-disguised amazement as they see us streaking towards them with the bogies dancing, the exhaust roaring and the connecting rods and piston just a blurr. I always spare moment or two passing Bicester just to see those looks. The firing is lighter now for a few miles even though we maintain our speed We continue to increase speed until we are almost on 100 mph. Unfortunately we can't say that we have exceeded the ton because the speedo, which only goes up to 100mph starts to have a fit of the trembles between about 97 and 100.

We fly though Blackthorn and Brill, to shut off before Haddenham in order to slow down to 35mph at Ashendon Junction. Again this is a bad place to slow down because it is a climb again up through Princess Risborough. Even so we can soon gain on the 35 or 40 which we come down to passing Ashendon and hammer them back up to 55 or 60 so that we quickly see Princess Risborough approaching. Again we pick up speed quickly but there is not enough time to reach very high speed down Saunderton because we once again have to slow down to 45mph round West Wycombe, and 35 at High Wycombe. Unbelievably the sticks are on again at High Wycombe and we pull slowly though the platform and up to the Box. The Bobby looks sheepish but protests that he has been given wrong information, "They told me you were 12 minutes late leaving Banbury and you had been stopped so I reckoned I could let that parcels go, I don't know where they get these stories from".

"The were quite right", Jack informed him, "We stood for 12 minutes at Banbury waiting for something to clear". The Signalman looks even more confused now to Jacks delight.

"He wont stop you again once I get the road", said the Bobby, clearly not knowing whether we are joking or not because to lose 12 minutes standing is like losing 15 by the time the train is moving again and he's finding it hard to believe that we have made that up between Banbury and his box. Shortly he pulls the stick off and waves us goodbye and Jack lays into them again because there is one more chance for a fast run before we finally shut off for Old Oak Common. The Castle responds again and we roar our way through the cutting and the short tunnel gathering speed through Beaconsfield, Seer Green and Gerards Cross. By the time the cutting sides fall away we are once more doing over 80mph. As we pass Denham we are nearing 90mph. Approaching Ruislip Jack lifts the regulator to give her a final roaring blast through and slams the regulator shut. I already have the fire blacked over and the firehole doors wide open, before filling the shovel with water to wash my hands.

That done I light a fag, sit down on the seat and enjoy the suburbs of the Greatest City in the world flashing by. Ruislip Gardens, Northholt, Greenford, we are streaking alongside the underground now overtaking their stoppers. Park Royal, Acton and Jack is putting the Brake in to slow down to 30 at

Old Oak Common where we join the main line to the West Country and pass Old Oak Common Shed which provides all the engines and men for the crack West Country trains. Once clear of the bend Jack picks them up again to steam gently and quietly past the ever more crowded areas of London, Westbourne Park, Royal Oak and slowly into Paddington.

As we finally stop a few yards short of the stop block the world seems to fall quiet and the excitement is over for a while. The Runner (Station Supervisor) comes up and protests that we were supposed to be at least 15 minutes late, "Well, it's nothing to us to make up 15 minutes", said Jack with a nice touch of nonchalance. The Runner gives us a look which means "Don't Bullshit me" and walks away. Jack laughs, he's not bothered whether we are believed or not, we know that we have done it, it's a beautiful summers evening, and we have had the satisfaction, the excitement and the downright pleasure of an almost perfect trip to London.

TOM

It was Spring 1914, Tom sauntered along Stafford Rd. His mates rode their bikes alongside, circling and weaving, pushing and bantering in the manner of lively young men. They'd all been on the 'tip' or as it was properly known, the coal stage. Their job was the coaling of steam engines. This was plain for anyone to see by the colour of their hands and faces. They all sported a generous coating of coal dust. This dust rose from their clothes in choking clouds as they pushed and jostled each other in mock battle. Shouting and laughing like the bubbling young idiots they were.

As Tom turned towards Stafford St, his mates rode towards Dunstall Rd and as they did they waved and shouted at Tom "Go and get yourself washed, you filthy sod." Tom replied, without looking back, it was one short, rude word! Although normally a very clean lad, he was not that anxious to rid himself of the night's dirt. He was quite proud of his black hands and face he wore his coat of coal dust like a badge of merit. He was a worker at last, a man of some importance.

Tom was an alert, no-nonsense product of the back streets of Wolverhampton. When he spoke his voice was sharp, his words were few, his manner aggressive and terse. He gave an impression of angry disillusionment with everything about him, of impatience with anything but immediate and productive action. Only in his secret mind was there room for romance, kindness or love.

He walked past the rows of doors and windows, broken every now and then by a dingy entry. It was all cosy and familiar, somehow, he had walked such streets all his life, he stretched and yawned as he savoured the morning air. It was one of those spring mornings when the air was full of the promise of summer. It was unusually mild but just cool enough to cleave the nostrils with the scent and freshness of the new day.

Tom was 17 years of age and in that short time had seen more rows and fights, more of the seamy, horrid side of human nature than most of us see in lifetime. He was weary and heartily sick of all that, and sensed the promise of better things to come. As long as he could remember, he had only wanted to be one of two things either a locomotive fireman (with the promise of being a driver), or a bargee. Both jobs involved travel and Tom had listened to the yarns of travelling men all his life. In his mind's eye he would see engines speeding across the countryside, the same countryside traversed by the winding canal with its' horse-drawn boats wending their way through scenes of rural peace and beauty. It was these private and romantic notions that drew him to a job in transport. The boats seemed to offer more freedom and fresh air, but the speed and excitment of the trains, their connections with far away holiday places and the uniforms and camraderie of the locomotive staff attracted him most. Besides all that, he had lived near to a Great Western engine driver who liked Tom and he had spoken for him. Only by being 'spoken for' was it possible to join staff at Stafford Rd loco department.

Now all that had been done and Tom was a GWR engine cleaner. To become a fireman, he had to undergo an extensive physical examination and a simple intelligence test, and he felt quietly confident of passing both. He still couldn't believe his luck for, as his parents never tired of telling him, it was a much sought-after job. Once a man entered the 'line of promotion' he was assured of a job for life with better than average pay. But above all, the thought of climbing aboard one of those steel monsters as the 'fireman' filled him with a sense of considerable importance. He saw himself and his driver pushing their way along a crowded platform, going to relieve the crew of some long distance train bound for, say Weymouth, Bournemouth or perhaps Plymouth, Penzance or St Ives.

Tom felt that they would be the focus of all attention for they were the men who would 'get them there'. He couldn't imagine anyone wanting any other job.

As he made his way up Stafford St, he was in a happy and contented frame of mind. There was a nice ring to 'finishing off nights'. As he passed the Elephant and Castle, he noticed that it was open. He could have gone in for a rum and coffee but it was not his style. He had seen too much of the misery and poverty brought about by drunkeness to be attracted to a pub so early in a morning.

He felt the coins in his pocket. He had quite a few bob saved already, so later after some sleep he might stroll down for a pint and a chat, but there was no way that beer would dominate him or empty his pocket, that was certain.

He was not keen to go straight home to bed as this would undoubtedly break the spell of this lovely morning. It was only just past 6 am and most people were still in bed. The streets and yards off Stafford St were strangely silent. Tom sauntered down Herbert St towards the goods yard; a sudden clatter of wagon buffers shattered the quiet as an engine backed on to a train. Along Great Western St were the stables that housed the great horses which pulled the many railway carts. He watched as a carter led his massive horse clattering and snorting on to the cobbled yard. It was a sight he had seen a hundred times before but now he was a worker himself, an insider 'coming off nights'.

The carter looked up and saw Tom. "Morning mate" he shouted. Tom replied and it felt good. On he strolled as far as Lock St. He couldn't resist a peep at the barges that he knew would be tied up near the top lock. So he pulled himself onto the top of the wall in Southampton St and sat looking down on the canal.

He could just see the water and the cabin of a boat through a gap in the sheds. The back of the barge was almost covered by a tarpaulin but this had been pushed back on to the side opposite the towpath, leaving the near side open to Tom's gaze.

He was looking into the confined but cosy space behind the cabin. Like many other boats, it was newly painted in bright colours. A towel hung over a small line, gleaming horse-brasses hung either side of the cabin door and a shining copper kettle completed the clean, cosy private place.

From somewhere near, the delicious aroma of bacon cooking drifted on the cool, still air. To Tom with his young and healthy appetite for food and life, it all seemed a bit like Utopia. Suddenly a young woman appeared from the cabin. Long blonde hair hung down her back, she had a carefree, happy face with eyes full of fun and excitement. Her top half, which was about all Tom could see, was covered by a thin, sleeveless vest. She was pouring hot water from the copper kettle into a bowl, obviously preparing for a wash. As she poured, the steam from the bowl rose through the streaming sunlight and for a moment or two she was almost completely hidden from Tom's gaze. As the steam gradually cleared so she was revealed leaning over the bowl but without her vest. Her full soft breasts moved as she washed her hands and arms. Tom's eyes almost popped as she began to soap her breasts looking down on them with a faint but unmistakable smile of satisfaction. Tom's emotions were on fire, temples pounded, cheeks blazed, his whole sexual being was excited.

The intense admiration that his mind had for her lovely face and flowing hair was outraged by the wild erotic sensations which the sight of her bare breasts unleashed. He was experiencing an emotional maelstrom unlike anything he'd known before. He had never been keen on 'peeping Tom'

56

and often wished that peeping Tom had been peeping Bill, Harry or Jim anything except Tom. But now, here he was, a real peeping Tom and no mistake. Not that he had meant to be, he was more of a victim than a villain.

As he sat in silent concentration, a man appeared from the cabin and stood behind this lovely girl. Tom's heart leapt. A third emotion joined the love and lust fighting in his breast it was fear. Most bargees could be aggressive and violent at any time, but to find a filthy peeping Tom ogling his young wife at her toilet, God only knows what might happen! By now Tom knew he should go. Commonsense and decency said he should go. Sheer, naked cowardice said he should go. BUT HE BLOODY-WELL COULDN'T GO!

The young bargee yawned and stretched. His muscles almost burst his shirt. He seemed to look in Tom's direction. Tom's heart missed a beat, but he stayed frozen where he was. The bargee was not alarmed. He was standing in bright sunlight while Tom sat in the shadow of the buildings, his black figure all but invisible. The girl was drying herself now, her towelled hands gently caressing those luscious breasts.

Tom's eyes almost parted company as he tried not to miss one single glimpse of flesh or nipple and at the same time, keep his eye on the bargee. The young woman threw down the towel and breathed deeply of the morning air. The brilliant morning sun lit her curving figure and gave poor Tom another hot flush. The bargee now moved close behind her, his massive arms encircled her, his great hands gently, tenderly caressed her breasts. Tom's temples pounded, his poor overheated frame could barely stand the strain, his safety valve was about to pop. The fear was still with him. He saw the gentle way those massive hands caressed the woman. But he was in no doubt what those same hands would do if they once landed on his dirty collar. The bargee pulled the girl closer, she leaned back and looked up at him in sweet submission.

It was a scene of beauty and fulfilment, far removed from Tom's previous experience. He knew a fair bit about sex. He knew it often involved rows and drunken violence, sometimes it involved money. He'd seen it bought and sold and fought over. In fact he cringed at the thought of it all. But this was completely different, in another world really, and it sent his senses reeling. The girl turned towards her lover and they embraced passionately, then she pushed him gently away, a mischievous smile on her lips and in her eyes. His face took on a similar look as if they shared some wonderful and incredibly joyful secret. She moved back into the cabin, her smiling face challenged him to follow. He moved slowly after her and they disappeared from view.

Tom felt weak and drained. He was like a man who had seen the open door of heaven just a step away, only to have it shut in his face. The girl's tinkling laugh and her lover's deep chuckle mingled and echoed up off the quiet water. Tom dropped from the wall onto shaky legs.

The morning was still as beautiful but somehow it had changed and Tom had changed with it. Although he would rarely speak of it, he would never forget the magic of this morning or the tenderness and beauty of the scene he had just witnessed. For it spoke to him of true, clean, wonderful love.

All his life from now on he would see this handsome young couple. She at the tiller, while he led his horse along a towpath fringed with meadows and beneath towering trees. Or moored by silent moonlit fields, nothing of humanity for miles but the tiny gleam of light from their boat. He saw them waking to the morning sunlight, standing naked and alone, children of nature, safe in their Arcadian world where all was love and peace and joy.

Even at seventeen years of age, Tom was too much of a realist to be unaware of the pitfalls that faced such an idyllic relationship. The repeated pregnancies, the grinding poverty and drudgery, the drunkenness and violence. All this he'd seen too often in his young life and wondered how any couple could survive such things. But somehow he felt that this couple could and should survive it all.

In the passing years he'd sometimes see some hard-faced boatie woman shrieking at her barefoot brats and realise that he might be looking at his nubile beauty of years before. Even this didn't mar the memory of that glorious spring morning. Tom just hoped it wasn't her, hoped that life had dealt more gracefully with her and her lover than it had with so many of their fellow water-gypsies.

He had hoped that they had the strength and love to make a life that reflected at least a little of the peace and joy it first promised. But whether it did or not made no difference, it opened the door for Tom. It gave him hope and a firm belief in love and goodness. That no-one was guaranteed such things he knew only too well but now he knew they were there and within his grasp.

As the years went by, many other happenings and many other people would help him to understand more of what life was all about. But nothing and no one did half as much to help Tom cast off the dark horrors of his early life than did that young couple aboard their barge on that magic morning.

He never spoke these exact words or expressed these exact feelings. When he spoke of these events his manner was awkward and his descriptions characteristically short, leaving much to the imagination. But to those who knew and liked him, the enormous effort needed by a man of his nature and background to even speak of such things was proof positive of its immense importance to him. He couldn't use fancy phrases but he knew when someone would understand and that saved a wealth of explanation. He had more native commonsense than to tell of it to those who would laugh or add crude and scoffing sexual comments; he wouldn't have told many folks at all. In fact for all I know, I could be the only one he did tell, but I understood and Tom knew it.

CONCLUSION

Brunel's Great Western Railway marched from Wolverhampton to London and Oxford, Penzance, South and North Wales, Crewe and Birkenhead. It also wound its' way over countless lovely branch lines, and we had a passport to a large slice of it. As we look back now, our minds surely fill with memories and impressions that were common to us all. Pictures appear in the mind's eye, crowding one after another endlessly. All of them grand in their own way, all equally important to us. Many have gone forever, but many more remain. The hills and valleys, towns and villages that we knew and looked on with affection that comes from long familiarity and involvement; farms and farmers that we saw so often and knew so well, yet never knew their names. The endless blossom fields of the Vale of Evesham. The winding river Tern and the massed rhododendrons of the Crewe branch. Embankments near Lapworth ablaze with the strange green light of glow worms.

A sea of heads at Snow Hill Station as happy, excited holiday makers thronged onto the platforms in a never ending stream that no amount of empty trains would stem. Hop pickers lining the stations of the West Midland Line, Bilston, Daisy Bank, Princes End and Tipton. Whole families with everything but the wall paper, everyone happy, excited, full of fun; and crowds of children (always there were children) thrilled out of their little minds, shouting with delight at the sight of the engine drawing the train that was to take them on their long awaited adventure.

The birch woods and wild sweet peas of Cosford. Hoar frost thickly coating the trees across the Madeley Branch, glistening in the bright, crisp dawn of a mid-winter's day. Looking down on Darby's Forge pool in beautiful Coalbrookdale. The River Severn at Buildwas and reaching back and forth at Cressage and Cound, or as we crossed and recrossed it at Belvedere and Worcester. The Vale of Llangollen from Cefn Viaduct, a dizzy height from the winding Dee on the valley floor. The golden ball on green Saunderton Hill.

The great sweep of the Line as we passed Filton Junction and raced towards Bristol. Bristol, the gateway to the West that promised golden beaches, rocky cliffs and conjured up magic names like

Teignmouth, Penzance, Dartmouth, Truro, Plymouth, St Ives. We never went there on the footplate, but we had their scent and flavour somehow as we waved the holiday excursions off.

In our minds eye we can walk again the silent lamplit streets and once more ride the deck of the iron horse across moonlit fields. Open cabs kept us close to the wind and weather from the icy cutting blast of winter to the scented breeze of a summer's day. It was just the two of us, driver and mate, sometimes at loggerheads it's true, but more often as friends; enjoying the freedom, the fun and achievement of it all, accepting the discomfort, difficulties, and occasionally the agony of it, together.

Most of my mates were great, one or two were just mates, and at least one was a real bastard. Well, best forget all that now, eh. Someone has said that to know all is to forgive all. I'm sure there's a great truth there.

I certainly couldn't profess to know all, but I do know a lot more and understand a lot more now than I did all those years ago. I certainly don't hate or even dislike the memory of anyone any more, so I must have learned to forgive a little. How I would love to be able to go back and shake the hands of some of those men once more and tell them what they meant to me then; to find the words and thoughts that seemed to blow away at the time in the gusting winds of a young man's selfish activity, and to say "Thanks mates, for the time of my life".

Acknowledgements

My acknowledgments for the co-operation of Ted Body,
Ian Howard, Roger Russell and Andy Hornett of Moreton Print Shop.

Also the late Bill Lines, Sid Clapham and Frank Jeavons.

Copies of this publication can be obtained from
G.Brown, 89 Crossland Crescent,Tettenhall, Wolverhampton WV6 9LA

Printed by Moreton Community Printshop, Wolverhampton (01902) 558280